PETER FRANZ RENNER

THE INSTRUCTOR'S SURVIVAL KIT A HANDBOOK FOR TEACHERS OF ADULTS

SECOND EDITION

WHAT A TEAM:

Design & production coordination	: Michael Kluckner
Editing & proofreading	: Christine Allen
Illustrations & cover design	: Gerhard Renner
Page-by-page layout	: Peter Renner
Typesetting	: Chimo Graphics
Printing & binding	: Hignell Printing

Cataloguing in Publication Data:

Renner, Peter F., 1943-
   The Instructor's Survival Kit

Includes bibliographical references and index.
ISBN 0-9690465-1-0

1. Teaching.   2. Adult Education.   I. Allen, Christine.
II. Training Associates Limited.   III. Title.
LC5219.R45   1983   371.1'02   C82-006771-X

Training Associates Ltd.,
Publishers & Consultants,
P.O. Box 58246 Station "L"
Vancouver, B.C., Canada V6P 6E3.
[604] 263-7091.
Printed in Canada.

Introduction to Second Edition

This is the second edition of The Instructor's Survival Kit. When I put together the first edition, in 1977, I intended it to be no more than a collection of handout material for people attending my "train the trainer" workshops. Now, five years and 9,000 copies later, the Kit has become widely accepted by instructors working in company training departments, community colleges, universities, public service and volunteer organizations.

Several dozen organizations have purchased the Kit in large quantitites for use in their own instructional skills development programs. The Kit has found a home on trainers' bookshelves coast-to-coast in Canada and the United States. Several copies managed to make their way to Australia, the Caribbean, the Middle East, Hong Kong, and Europe.

After much agonizing and many inevitable delays, the second, completely re-written edition is completed. It remains faithful to the goal stated on the introductory page to the first edition: ". . . to help you keep your head above water during the first few sessions you teach." Furthermore, it is still "not a book about the theories of adult education, but a practical, how-to book that must be used to be useful."

Sixty percent of the old material has been re-worked and reads so much better now. The rest is new material. The combination of old and new and many aspects of the arrangement and wording reflect the comments of several colleagues "out there" who took the trouble to write and send specific criticism and materials. Some of their material entered directly into this Kit (and is acknowledged where it appears); other information has been combined with my own words. I'd specifically like to thank Brigham Card, Rick Childerhouse, Les Ellenor, Alan Green, Sean Gregg, Reg Herman, Wes Hickey, Ed Kemps, Dianne Morrison, Patricia Moore, John Owen, M.J. Perez, Susan Reuthe, David Tickner, Veronica Timmons, David Terrell and Maret Watson for their contributions.

My special thanks go to Michael Kluckner and Christine Allen who, aside from being design coordinator and editor respectively, provided me with a safe haven throughout this project and have become my friends.

3M, the Minnesota Mining and Manufacturing Co., gave permission to reproduce on pages 85-87 their copyrighted material on the overhead projector. Our limited reproduction permission (page 2) is inspired by University Associates of San Diego.

A note on the use of the third person pronoun. I deliberated—should I say 'he' or 'she'?; should I construct my sentences in such a way to avoid the problem?; perhaps write 's/he'? My solution to the puzzle was to mix up the references to genders and use 'he' at times, 'she' at others. I hope no one will be offended.

It is my wish that you enjoy this book, that it will become your friend in need, that you pass it to your colleagues (or better, ask them to buy their own).

peter renner

How To Use This Book

The **Kit** is divided into two parts. The first 88 pages are the prime survival tools—techniques that you can use at random to break the ice with a new group, to present information, to involve learners and to utilize standard visual aids. Part two, pages 89 to 132, might be called the post-survival material. Here you can find information to help you develop your interpersonal and planning skills.

There is rarely a "right" way to use the techniques described in the **Kit.** My suggestions for time required, materials needed, group size, and step-by-step instructions are flexible. You must decide when and how to use them; please adapt anything in these pages to suit your style and your teaching situation.

Table of Contents

"Training is a bane for some, salvation for others, but for most it is misunderstood and misused. Many...identify training with the process to teach dogs to sit, roll over, and retrieve."

Irwin R. Jahns. "Training in Organizations." In S.M. Grabowski & Associates, **Preparing Educators of Adults.** San Francisco: Jossey-Bass, 1981. p. 94.

The Instructor as Facilitator

Adult education plays an important role in shaping and developing the people in our society. Within each school, training program or company seminar there is a number of teachers (instructors) who are responsible for guiding the learning activities of the adult students. The teacher appears to be the single most vital influence in the system. We often forget the facts and figures of a course taken long ago, but many of us remember certain teachers who have been particularly helpful—or hindering—in our efforts to learn. If a person learns to associate either a school, course, or the instructor with strong feelings of anxiety, frustration or inadequacy then that school, course, or teacher has not been effective.

The instructor and the learner are in a special type of temporary helping relationship. The learner comes because he feels a need to grow, discover, increase skills and knowledge, and has decided that a school setting would be the best place to do so. The learner feels that the instructor will be knowledgeable and skilful in providing the service. The instructor is there because he feels that he possesses the subject knowledge and teaching skills required to fulfil the needs of the learner. Traditionally, this situation then forms the basis for a dependency relationship, with the instructor doing the telling and the learner doing the listening. Many educators today view the instructor/learner relationship more as one of interdependency, because neither party can enact his role without the participation of the other. Or, said another way, a teacher can no more teach without a learner than a salesperson can sell without a purchaser. We can only facilitate his efforts to learn. This departure from traditional approaches to teaching places joint responsibility on the instructor and the learner. The learner, not the instructor, is the protagonist in search of change, new and improved skills and knowledge. The learner's task is to decide how this information fits into his life and why.

The moment the instructor takes over these choices and responsibilities a dependent relationship develops. The learner looks to the instructor for solutions. In fact, the entire responsibility for the success or failure of the course is, in this case, placed on the instructor's shoulders, and many instructors actually see their role as being responsible for, and in charge of, the learner's learning. This assumption disregards the learning adult's right and responsibility to manage his or her own life. It also inhibits the kind of learning students must do to successfully "complete" the course; to go back to their personal and work situations and use whatever new knowledge and behavioral changes that have occurred.

To be effective as a facilitator an instructor ought to possess certain basic skills:
• adequate expertise in the subject area.
• some general knowledge of learning theory, and technical (instructional) skills to present the material in a learnable fashion.
• a well-developed repertoire of interpersonal skills through which he can establish, maintain and develop effective relationships and an atmosphere conducive to learning.

Most teachers of adults are selected because they have displayed a sufficient mastery of the subject they are to teach. This applies equally to company training programs, community agencies, recreation centers and continuing education classes at high schools or colleges. However, mastering the subject matter is a prerequisite to good teaching but is no guarantee of it.

Carl Rogers lists his "Guidelines for Facilitation" which have influenced my own development as a teacher.[1]

1. The facilitator is largely reponsible for setting the initial mood or climate of the program.
2. The facilitator helps to elicit and clarify the purposes of the individuals in the class as well as the more general purposes of the group.
3. He relies upon the desire of each student to implement those purposes which have meaning to him as the motivational force behind significant learning.
4. He endeavours to organize and make easily available the widest possible range of resources for learning.
5. He regards himself as a flexible resource to be utilized by the group.
6. As the classroom climate becomes established, the facilitator is increasingly able to become a participant learner, a member of the group, expressing his views as an individual.
7. He takes the initiative in sharing himself with the group—his feelings as well as his thoughts—in ways which neither demand nor impose but represent simply a personal sharing which the student may take or leave.
8. Throughout the course, he remains alert to expressions indicative of deep or strong feelings.
9. He endeavours to recognize and accept his own limitations as a facilitator of learning.

[1]Carl Rogers. **Freedom to Learn.** Columbus, Ohio: C.E. Merrill Publ. 1969. pp. 164-166.

Techniques Chart

Here are some suggestions for the use of the teaching techniques described on the following pages. Depending on what you want to do (A to G) some are more useful than others.

A— To help the learner develop knowledge about facts, figures, concepts, make generalizations about experience, internalization of information.

B— To help the learner develop understanding...apply information and generalizations; relate theory to the real world, make connections between classroom learning and learner's previous experience.

C— To help the learner develop skills in performing certain tasks, operating equipment, handling tools, practising new behaviors.

D— To help the learner develop attitudes towards issues, situations, problems; adopt new feelings through experiencing greater success with them than with old feelings (and attitudes and behaviors).

E— To help the learner develop values...adopt and put in order of priority certain beliefs.

F— To involve learners actively in the learning process through participation.

G— To obtain feedback on the learner's thoughts and feelings about what is going on.

Techniques	A	B	C	D	E	F	G	page
Expectations Survey	*	*	*	*	*	*	*	29
Learning Contracts	*	*	*	*	*	*		33
Ass'd Read & Research	*				*	*		67
Lecture	*							37
Buzz Groups		*			*	*	*	35
Circle Response	*	*			*	*	*	41
Circles of Knowledge	*	*				*	*	43
Spend-a-Penny						*		45
Speedy Memo						*	*	49
Brainstorming	*	*				*		47
Role Playing		*	*	*	*	*		61-65
Discussions		*	*	*	*	*	*	51
Critical Incident		*	*	*	*	*		57
Panel Debate	*					*		71
Debate Forum	*					*		73
Field Trip	*	*				*		75
Field Project	*	*	*	*		*		77
Warmups						*		17-27
Learning Journal		*	*	*	*	*	*	79
Evaluation Tools						*	*	121-128

And Thus Spake Malcolm Knowles

Knowles coined the term 'andragogy' to describe the theory and practice of adult education, in contrast to 'pedagogy,' which is concerned with the education of children. He is the champion of learner-oriented teaching as reflected in his "foundation stones of modern adult learning theory":

• adults are motivated to learn as they experience needs and interests that learning will satisfy; therefore, these are the appropriate starting points for organizing adult learning activities.

• adults' orientation to learning is life-centered; therefore, the appropriate units for organizing adult learning are life situations, not subjects.

• experience is the richest resource for adults' learning; therefore, the core methodology of adult education is the analysis of experience.

• adults have a deep need to be self-directed; therefore, the role of the teacher is to engage in a process of mutual inquiry with them rather than to transmit his or her knowledge to them and then evaluate their conformity to it.

[1]Knowles, M. **The Adult Learner: A Neglected Species.** *2nd edition. Houston: Gulf. 1978. p. 31.*

Instructional techniques are the wide variety of approaches that you have at your disposal to present the course material to your learners. Before you decide on a specific technique, consider these factors:

Is the technique suited to your objectives?

What do you want to accomplish by using it? Is it to entertain, relax, impress, arouse, stimulate or inform your learners? Are you planning to have them acquire new skills and new information or are you exploring attitudes and feelings? Each area has its own appropriate teaching technique. A *demonstration-practice* session is more effective if students are to acquire specific *skills*. Developing or changing *attitudes* about something may be best accomplished through a *role play* followed by a discussion. For the acquisition of *technical knowledge*, buzz groups may not be the appropriate technique—a *lecture*, or *assigned reading* is probably better.

What can you do well?

Base your instruction on your strengths! Stick to techniques that you are comfortable with and venture into new ones with caution. When you do try something new, you might tell your class: "I want to try something new this morning. I've seen it work with similar groups but haven't actually tried it myself (or only once before). So, hang in there and see if we can make it work." The success of the new technique now becomes the shared responsibility of all the people in the room.

Can your students use the technique?

Do they know how to make the best of this teaching technique? Have they ever been exposed to it? Was their previous experience a good one? In some cases, such as small group discussions, projects and practice sessions, you may have to spend some time explaining the procedure and advantages of a technique before it can be used effectively. You may have studied law and be familiar with the Socratic approach to questioning, or be well acquainted with case studies of business management topics. Your learners may or may not share your expertise and enthusiasm. You may have to assist them in learning how to learn by your particular method.

What are your learners' expectations?

Pet techniques can be hazardous to your health. I once spent many sessions "battling" with trainee instructors to make them adopt my style of teaching/learning. I had decided that a mixture of discussion and reflection would be best for them. Only when I made the problem the answer could I begin to enjoy my work again. The problem? My students were reluctant to discuss and reflect, mostly because they had had little previous experience to base such activities upon. The answer? I asked them early in the course how they felt the course should be conducted. They expected to be given "lots of information," some "practical hints," my own "tricks of the trade" and some help with teaching problems. The moment I switched from my pet techniques the battle was over; I could rest more easily and my students, so they said, learned more.

What are your physical restraints?

It is virtually impossible to use group discussions in a fixed-setting lecture room. But it is possible to ask two people to turn to the two behind them and form a "buzz group."

Role playing could also be used to give participants a chance to experience the world from someone else's viewpoint. If you wish to be close to your students and establish personal rapport, a 200-people lecture theatre could frustrate your efforts. An inspection of the assigned room may influence your choice of technique; so will class size, time limits and a crowded course outline.

Set the stage

"Next week we'll try something different. My last class enjoyed it when we . . ." Or, "Tonight I have planned a change in your routine." By telling your students what to expect, how they could benefit from involvement and how we are going to proceed, you can reduce their apprehension, particularly if this new thing asks learners to change from being passive to being active. Some instructors like to "spring" a new technique on their class without warning, counting on just that anxiety to bring about some action. I do this only with a group that knows me and when I have time to discuss the new technique afterwards.

Domains of Learning

Educational theorists state that learning is not one process, but can be categorized into **domains**, depending on what is to be learned:

1. **cognitive,** which deals with the recall or recognition of knowledge and the development of intellectual abilities and skills;

2. **affective,** which describes changes in attitude and values, and the development of appreciations and adequate adjustment;

3. **psychomotor,** which has to do with the development of manipulative skills, involving tools, machinery, procedures and techniques.

Bloom, B.S. et al. **Taxonomy of Educational Objectives.** *Handbook I. New York: McKay, 1956. p 7.*

Never limit your teaching strategies just because you teach in a room that has fixed rows of chairs, or only chairs with attached desks. For the time you and your class meet this is your room and you have the power to do whatever is necessary to enhance learning through good seating arrangements.

Many of the techniques described in this book can be used with immovable chair arrangements. In all other situations it takes only a minute's work by you and your group to rearrange the room. Please think of the people that follow you, including the cleaning staff, and return everything to its original place.

If you teach mostly towards the **acquisition of knowledge** (information, concepts, facts) area, the use of tables, desk tops, or some other writing surface is probably a must. (One theory is that the desk top has the additional advantage of hiding about half of a person's body, thus providing some sense of security and allowing for higher concentration on the material to be learned.)

Here are some set-ups you can use with conventional furniture:

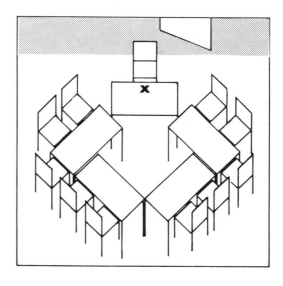

Everyone can look at everyone else while speaking and listening. The X is your spot and behind you is a flip-chart or chalkboard. Most of the comments will probably flow towards you at the "head of the table." Watch who sits at the other end of the table, because the person(s) there may have a similar power position. This arrangement makes it awkward to use the overhead projector.

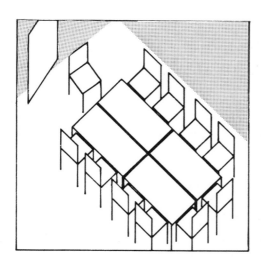

The closest thing to a round table using rectangular tables. The more distance between tables the more formal the interactions tend to be at the beginning. Here, almost everyone is in view but it is probably impractical for more than 25 people.

Cleaner lines than above, but no designated head table for the instructor. This is useful if all the material is in front of the learners (no chalkboard or overhead projections) and an all-group discussion is part of the learning strategy.

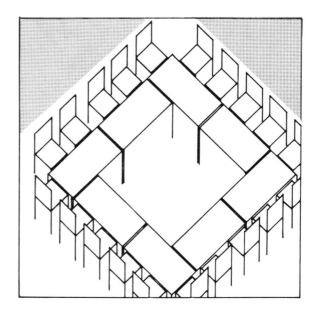

Lecture setting for large groups. Ideally each person has a little desk top to write on (lap-held clipboards become cumbersome). The slightly semi-circular arrangement gives more harmony to the large mass of people all facing in your direction. If the seats are movable, leave a center aisle for better access, and knee space between rows. If there are more chairs than people, encourage people to fill the room starting at the front.

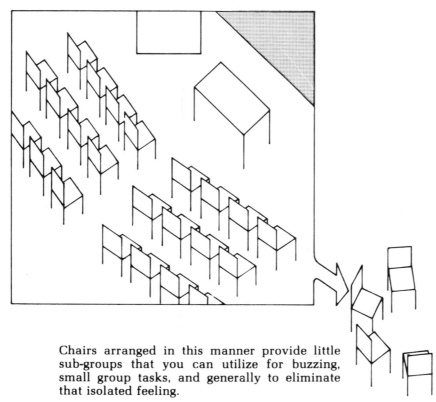

Chairs arranged in this manner provide little sub-groups that you can utilize for buzzing, small group tasks, and generally to eliminate that isolated feeling.

If **skill acquisition** is the main purpose of your activities, it will limit the size of your group. Everybody must be able to clearly see what you are demonstrating and have all their questions answered as they follow you step-by-step.

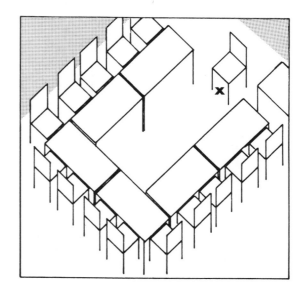

X marks the spot where you either sit or stand to give your demonstration. If imitation or practice by the students follows, this arrangement allows you to move in and out of their work areas, give individual attention and keep an eye on all.

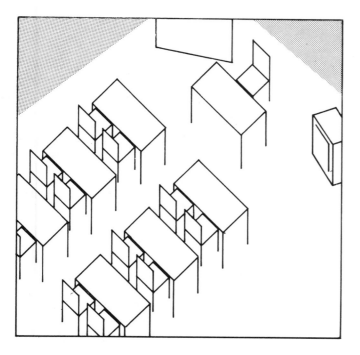

In certain shop or laboratory settings the instructor is provided with either an overhead mirror or a video camera. This allows the students who cannot view the demonstration directly at least to see it "second-hand."

When your main focus is on **attitude development**, tables may be a hindrance. I am thinking of courses (or parts thereof) where the emphasis is on feelings, attitudes, values, opinions, prejudices, etc. People seem to have more difficulty making personal statements while concealed behind desks. If you wish to encourage people to "show themselves" instead of making abstract statements, the removal of tables will set the stage very nicely. If the atmosphere of your course is informal, it would be best if everyone could sit on the floor or cushions, or on the carpet.

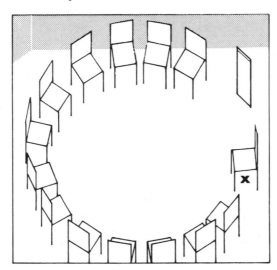

Circular arrangements are preferable in attitudinal learning situations. X is your spot and indicates that all contributions will be given equal value. The traditional "up front" power position would not encourage personal statements and learning.

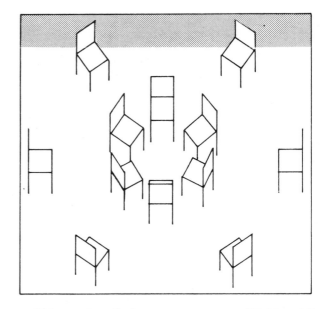

This one is called group-on-group or "fishbowl." The inner group is working on some problem-solving talk or discussing an issue or concern. The outer group is instructed to watch for certain behaviours in the inner group, and will later act as consultant and process-evaluator to it. To avoid one-upmanship, groups should be switched around. The instructor floats to give instructions, observe and keep time.

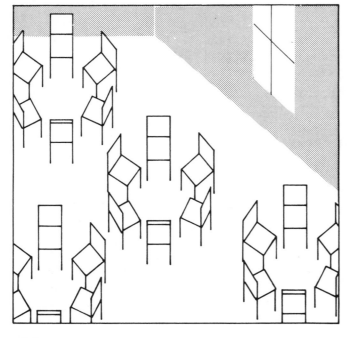

Several task or discussion groups work simultaneously and the instructor floats. Naturally, your course, your school, and your students will be different every time a course starts. The strategies that follow are very flexible and *must* be adapted to suit your situation. You may use them any way you see fit. Feel free to argue with the descriptions and comments, change them, enjoy them, and build on them.

Some get-acquainted activities are customary before a course starts but they can be a nuisance to both instructor and learners. Have you ever tried to start a group by having everyone introduce themselves and state their reasons for taking the course? What seems to happen is that the first person is caught off-guard, the next person immediately starts thinking about what to say and those at the end have been so busy rehearsing their statements in light of the previous (always more impressive) introductions, that they don't hear what other people have said. When their turn comes, they barely fumble through. There are many variations on this scenario.

Try to avoid putting people on the spot; remember that people are nervous when they appear in the classroom at the beginning of a course. They have many questions that need answers: What kind of course will this be (as dull, exciting, disappointing, heavy as the last one)? Who are the other people here? Do they know more or less about the subject than I do? Who is the instructor? Is that him over there talking to the attractive woman in the corner? Is he the one sitting at the center table with the pile of books, looking so very occupied and *knowledgeable*? Will I like it here? What is expected of me? Where is the washroom?

Warm-ups, get-acquainted and ice-breaking activities give the instructor a chance to settle in and get the feel of the group, but they should also help members of a class to:
- settle in and feel somewhat at home
- find out who else is there
- tell the others who they are (show off a bit)
- have their basic questions answered.

The activities described in the following pages have been used in a variety of adult education settings. They do not require special human relations training or knowledge, only sensitivity to and respect for the occasion, and the instructor's desire to get the course off to an enjoyable start. Basically, people learn better if they enjoy the learning. Making the classroom, the rest of the group and the instructor appear less strange can help create a warm, non-threatening environment for enjoyable learning. At the outset some sort of naming exercise is probably enough, plus some information on the course content, "rules" of the school, tests, readings, where the library is, etc. Often there will be some housekeeping chores to be completed (attendance books, texts, money for lab material, registration forms). Also, not all people will come at the same time and those coming late should not be made to feel they have missed out on something. At this stage learners tend to expect the instructor to impose structure on what could be slightly chaotic conditions.

These guidelines will help you in choosing which activities to use, how to use them, and in what order or combination. The sequence of activities should begin at a level of "self disclosure" that is not threatening, and should move at a gradual rate to more personal levels. Just how threatening these activities are is determined by *what* the students are asked to say, and to *whom*. To ask the learners what they would do with a lottery win of $20,000 is less threatening than to ask them how they feel about their mothers. Asking people to talk in front of a large audience is more threatening than asking them to do so in a smaller group.

Once things have settled down, the people who are in the wrong course have left, and everyone has a fairly good idea of the nature of the course and what it holds in store for them, you can introduce some getting-acquainted exercises. These activities are for sharing some information about "self" and helping learners find out who the members of the class are. This increases the level of trust and the degree of belonging to the class, and lets people discover the things they have in common. The naming exercise, mentioned previously, is just a start in this direction. Often people (and this includes myself as the instructor), barely remember all the names uttered in the heat of the first introduction.

Most educators agree that education should be relevant to the life of the adult learner. For learners to make connections between the course, subject and their own lives, they need opportunities to talk with each other about their lives and how the learning fits into them. This process requires more self-disclosure than is usually expected by adult students and their instructors. Using the activities that follow, you can help reduce anxiety and speed the process of opening up to each other. They will help adults learn new information, change attitudes and recognize feelings associated with the process of learning.

For more warm-up activities, see:
Sue Forbess-Green. **The Encyclopedia of Icebreakers.** 1982. San Diego: University Associates. (Includes 150 structured activities to assist trainees to get acquainted, to re-energize a group during "low" periods. The cost is a whopping US$66.20.

During the first session a great deal of information is thrown at your students. Some of them are old hands at it, they know what to expect, which questions to ask, and when to go into a light slumber without missing a thing. Others, probably quite new to being in school as adults, are bewildered and don't hear half of what you are telling them. If you think this is not true, just listen to some of the questions people ask you half-way through the course. "But I thought I told you back in May...." You did, but not everyone was listening. There were too many other things to consider and worry about.

Recommended To
- solve a problem
- discuss a case
- explore an issue
- make a list of ideas
- build something
- work on a project
- help break the ice for a new class.

Do not ask students to introduce themselves. Do not make a speech on what is going to happen in week four or what format you would like to see essays in, or what your philosophy of newt-breeding is, or how punctuality is one of your pet peeves, or what happened to you during your apprenticeship, etc. These might be interesting topics to talk about when there is need for a slower-paced moment but do not expect any important information to be comprehended by all listeners. Rather, do this: put a transparency on an overhead projector, or pin up a pre-designed poster, with this format (see below).

Stress that last point: "Don't be afraid to ask *any* question...there are no dumb questions in this course." Help the class break up into groups of not more than five people each, and allow them five minutes to make a list. Ask one person to be the recorder. If people have not met before, they most likely will begin their little group meeting with mutual introductions (or you might suggest they do).

After every group has a list (check by floating around the room), get a spokesperson for the group to ask you the first question. Stress again that any question is OK and allow one question per group at a time to avoid monopolizing.

Some of the best possible outcomes of this activity:
- a banding together of subgroups composed of people who, minutes ago, were complete strangers and now are less so. They also have obtained from you some of the information they wanted, and not necessarily what you chose to supply.
- by putting yourself in the "hot seat" you have demonstrated the possibility of shared power and equality between all the people in the room.

FORM GROUPS OF FOUR TO FIVE

DECIDE WHAT QUESTIONS YOU WANT TO ASK PETER ABOUT:

1. MY BACKGROUND
   MY EXPERIENCE
   MY PRESENT ACTIVITIES,
        ETC.

2. THE COURSE — ITS HOURS
   ITS CONTENTS
   TESTS
   PRACTICUM

PLEASE ASK ME ANY QUESTIONS THAT YOU FEEL ARE IMPORTANT TO YOU !!

This exercise takes less time than you may think; it is certainly quicker and more effective than a pep talk. If there is some information that people *must* have for use later in the course (examination schedule, essay format, reading assignments, field trip date) this is best given in a *handout* to be kept by the students.

Giving Instructions

Instructions must be *specific, understood,* and include a *time limit* for the completion of the task. Announcing the instructions verbally tends to create problems; not everybody hears or understands. Those who do immediately proceed to work and discuss, while others are still not sure what is going on. Still others may have heard, but need additional instructions or information. I have found it less time-consuming to write the task on a piece of newsprint, the chalkboard, the overhead projector or even on a handout. If you have planned the group activity in advance it should be written in advance (to save time in class).

Once the problem/task is understood by all people, announce a time limit for its completion. When first using small group activities with a new class, try to keep the *time limit* below seven minutes, depending on the complexity of the task. If it requires more time, break it into sub-tasks to allow for an opportunity to check on the progress at a certain point.

Thus, instructions could go like this: "Form groups of five persons each and, with one of you acting as a recorder, prepare a list of the steps your group would take to solve the 'x' problem. You have five minutes."

After four minutes announce the remaining one minute; if everyone is still working productively, announce an additional two minutes.

Physical Arrangements

During the first session and even after several sessions, people may find it easy enough to form groups of five, but they will not willingly change their seating arrangements. It probably feels safer to remain sitting in a row or at a desk, than to move around to face one another. One way to handle this is to put a quick diagram on the board explaining the desired layout.

Instructions are helpful: "Sit as closely together as you are comfortable. What is important is that you are facing each other so that each person can see and hear the others." After the first two or three such exercises, the brief announcement, "Please move to your usual working group of about five people" will quickly transform your class of 34 into seven effective learning groups.

For a description of the stages learning groups typically move through and to find techniques to assess and assist that development, see the excellent:

Gene Stanford. **Developing Effective Classroom Groups.** *New York: Hart 1977.*

Richard & Patricia Schmuck. **Group Processes in the Classroom.** *Dubuque, Iowa: W.C. Brown 1971.*

Asking your students to rearrange themselves into small groups of five to six people may seem a simple instruction but it often creates confusion. By anticipating some of the problems you can make full use of the advantages of small groups.

Advantages

- Lectures and other instructor-centered activities invite passivity on behalf of the learners but small group activities require and encourage activity.
- In small groups people have less chance to "hide" (cause for some anxiety) or to be "forgotten" (cause for a feeling of insignificance).
- People tend to speak up more freely in small groups than in front of a whole class.
- A certain amount of competition is created by giving the same task to a number of groups. This aids in keeping the groups "on task" and increases productivity.
- In a large class a person may feel little responsibility for the success of the course. In small group tasks he has a greater incentive to contribute.
- Individuals tend to work harder in small groups than in large ones.

Group Size

Dyads = two people
Only with people who know and trust each other would this size be of value. Research indicates that members tend to feel intensely responsible to one another, to avoid expressing disagreement or antagonism, and to feel obliged to adjust to the other's preferences and style of behavior. If one member withdraws, the group becomes ineffective.

Triads = three people
This is the minimum-sized group

where a coalition can form; the group (of two) can still function if one member withdraws or does not cooperate. Creative and innovative ideas are more likely to develop here than in a group of only two people.

Small Groups = two to five people
From all indications this seems to be the "ideal" size for a small task-oriented group. The advantages listed previously appear to have the best chance of fulfilment here.

Small Groups = six to ten people
Once you exceed five members per group, there is a tendency for sub-groups to form and go off on their own tangents. Members then complain of a lack of coordination, insufficient opportunity to have a say and poor use of time, and the accomplishments tend to be of poorer quality. Face-to-face interactions and the care and consideration that are associated with them become difficult if there are more than eight people. Personal statements are not made and people tend to experience less personal satisfaction and involvement with the group's activities.

See also: Matthew Miles, **Learning to work in Groups.** New York: Teachers College Press, 1970.

The Psychology of Small Group Behavior

Marvin Shaw has summarized research findings pertaining to group dynamics[1]. He describes the characteristics of individuals who compose the group as constituting a personal environment in which the group must operate. "People's manner of behaving, their typical reactions to others, and their skills and abilities determine not only their own behavior patterns, but also to a large extend the reactions of others to them as group members." [p. 154]

Shaw presents some plausible hypotheses about small group behavior. They include the following:

1. the total amount of participation in the group decreases with increasing group size.

2. the probability that a leader will emerge increases with increasing group size.

3. group members usually rate small groups more positively than larger groups.

4. the likelihood of conformity to a unanimous majority increases with increasing group size.

5. social participation increases with increasing chronological age.

6. group leaders tend to be older than other group members; there is a slight tendency for physically superior individuals to become leaders.

7. men tend to be more aggressive and more competitive in groups than women.

8. women communicate with eye contact more frequently than men.

9. the individual with special skills relative to the group teask usually is more active in the group, makes more contributions toward the task, and has more influence on group decisions.

10. the anxious group member inhibits group functioning, and (you guessed it) the well-adjusted member contributes to the group's functioning.

---

[1]Shaw, M.E. Group Dynamics. The Psychology of Small Group Behavior. New York: McGraw-Hill. 1976. pp 185-192.

Names are important to all of us. It is comforting to be addressed by name in a strange environment. Having one person introduce him/herself is fine but there are few people who will remember even half the names mentioned.

The stick-on type of tag with HELLO on it is a good beginning to the matching of names and faces. The problem with these tags is that they have a tendency to fall off people's clothing and they certainly will not re-appear for the second session.

Using double-folded sheets of paper or old computer cards as desk-top name cards is more useful. Have each person print (in bold letters) the name they want to be called on both sides of the card. Have brightly coloured felt pens on hand. This activity gets you past the awkward Mr./Mrs./Ms. first name/last name quandary. Also, the cards can be brought back for the next session.

Variations

★ Ask participants to put their present job, their company, or whatever might be relevant to the situation in small letters in the corners of the card.

★ Ask them to put on the inside "Only for you to see" the completion of these sentences:
—What I'd really like to do right now is . . . .
—I hope this course won't be . . . .
—What I would like to learn in this course includes . . . .

While this information is confidential at this stage, you may ask volunteers later on in the session or course to share it with the class. It is a technique to help members focus on their expectations, their present feelings and their hopes. It might also convey the notion that you care about these feelings and are aware of their presence.

Name Calling

This is a variation of the old go-around-naming routine. It is best done a couple of sessions after the initial introductions; perhaps halfway through the day or just before going home. Ask your class to bring their chairs around in a circle, or to sit on the table edges or the floor. You too must be part of the circle. Introduce the activity with: "We have been together for almost three sessions now and I have to admit I still don't know all of you by name. Remember the first night when we introduced ourselves? Well, I thought you would all like to play a game I remember playing when I was a kid. It goes like this: I'll start by telling you my name. Turn to the person on your right, repeat my name and add yours and so we will go around the circle. When your turn comes you have to try to repeat all the names before yours and then add your own. Don't worry about forgetting a name, you simply ask the person."

Allow for some reaction to your announcement of this activity, but don't hesitate to remind them "Well you know who has to do it all at the end . . ." (yourself!)

This perhaps sounds a bit dry (reciting names) but it is an easy way to:
- get everyone to speak up in the group
- increase the chance of people calling each other by name
- look at each other, and
- have a good laugh.

How To Remember Names

George Bell offers this advice for remembering names[1]:

1. Pay attention to the name. Hear it the first time, or ask the person to repeat it.

2. Repeat the name yourself. This will improve recall by 30%.

3. Use the name in conversation. Repetition will engrave the name in your long-term memory.

4. Observe the faces. Most of us can remember faces better than names, so really study the face and choose one outstanding detail.

5. Associate the name with the face. Form a mental picture, using an active image. Get the BELL to ring, the BYRD to fly, WATERS to gush.

6. Use the name when saying Good-bye. This final reinforcer also ensures that you know the name.

[1]From: **Training** Magazine. January 1979.

Each person is given a piece of paper (8 x 11) on which the heading **I AM...** is written in bold felt pen. Ask everyone to finish this statement in at least six different ways. An example you might want to show the class:

> **I AM...**
> -an engineer
> -a father
> -a stamp collector
> -feeling a bit silly
> -fun
> -a non-smoker

After everyone has finished ("No, you can't have more than six items!"), distribute a piece of masking tape to each person and have them attach their **I AM...** sheet to their front. You also do it. Then instruct the class to get up and move around to see who is there. They should spend at least 30 seconds with each person, reading and seeing who they are. No talking is allowed. Some people may need encouragement to get up, but play along and model your own instructions. You may have to remind people "No talking" which causes giggles and whispered conversations. People are talking to each other already!

After everyone has had a chance to circulate, ask them to hang their sheets on the wall "Our gallery." Invite people to have another look during the break or before going home. This activity makes for conversations on very safe topics: "So, you like stamp collecting too...?"

Variations

★Just hand everyone a blank piece of paper. Tear off pieces of masking tape and hang the tape over the edge of the tables within everyone's reach. Ask each person to put their name in bold letters at the top of the sheet (colored felt pens are an instructor's best friend).

Tell them: "I would like you to print five or six words ending with 'ing' on the sheet. They should tell something about yourself, who you are, what you like (reading, cooking, travelling, loving)."

Other possible word endings:

'able'—as in approachable, reasonable, capable

'ist'—as in optimist, realist, pianist, cyclist, specialist

'ful'—as in playful, frightful (?!), careful, hopeful, delightful.

Ask class members to attach the card to themselves (you are a member too), and mill about the room. You can try this either with "No talking for the first two minutes" or encourage them to stop and ask questions.

★I am a Resource:
This is similar to **"I AM..."** but the sheet has the above heading. Ask people to write on it all the things/areas/subjects they have some kind of expertise in. Stipulate whether or not it should be confined to the course content. Mention that this is a way of finding what backgrounds people have, that you are curious about the variety of people taking your course and are always surprised by the talents of adult students. Give some examples from your own sheet to get things rolling: "Brag a bit about yourself—you have my permission" (or, "that's an order!").

The sheet could look like this:

> **I AM A RESOURCE...**
> -own my own business
> -know about newt-breeding
> -am an electronics buff
> -ski a bit
> -speak Albanian
> -just bought my first house

Again, this could be a starting point for an *interview* or go-around for introductions. The information can be posted during the first session and then you keep the sheets. I have used the information to relate course material to specific people: "As a new house owner you probably know..."; "It's almost as rare as newt-breeding...."

Nice touch.

In my experience, the climate required for adults to learn best is one of trust, mutual support, respect and warmth. In such a climate the learner can feel comfortable about taking risks (by admitting ignorance, by trying out new behaviors, by asking what may seem like stupid questions) and become open to the opinions, ideas and contributions of others. He may also begin to see himself as a growing person, with the potential to help others learn, and to feel the excitement that comes with the discovery of new skills and knowledge.

Tom Boydell has described "five phases in the development of a learning community"[1]:

1. establishing appropriate climate
2. identifying needs
3. identifying resources
4. meeting needs
5. evaluation

You can find a combination of strategies in the KIT to assist you and your learners to move through all five phases.

---

[1]Boydell, T. **Experiential Learning.** Manchester, England: University of Manchester. 1976.

Ask the students to turn to one of their neighbors and blink to indicate that "You are now a team of two!" Everyone been blinked at? Now: "I'd like you to spend four minutes together and interview the other person. Find out at least three things (other than name) about your partner." Depending on the extent of your group's natural shyness, you might want to suggest: "Why are you taking this course? Where do you come from? What do you want to do when the course is finished?"

After the time is up (gauge it according to the amount of talking, but try to keep close to the announced limit), ask people to come back together as a class: "Now I'd like you each to introduce your partner, the person you have just interviewed." It is best to model an introduction yourself if you managed to team up with a partner: "I'd like you all to meet Siegfried Mueller, he comes from Albania and this is his first course. He. . . ." You could ask the introduced person to stand up briefly so that "we can all see each other." Thank everyone for their participation.

Variations

★ This involves three people and no assigned questions. Help your class to arrange themselves in triads, which should be dispersed about the room as much as possible to provide some privacy. If you use this exercise with an established class, you might ask members to form triads with the people they know least or with people they have never talked to. Then give instructions:

"Quickly name yourselves 'A', 'B' and 'C' so that I can give you further instructions.

"Person 'A', I'd like you to tell the other two people in your group as much about yourself and your reasons for being here (or expectations of this course) as you feel comfortable doing. You have two minutes.

"Then I'd like 'B' and 'C', who have just listened during the two minutes, to report back to 'A' what they have heard. You may also add anything that you assume 'A' said, or meant to say. 'A' should clarify so that each of you understands what 'A' is indeed saying.

"Then repeat the process, this time 'B' speaks first to 'C' and 'A' listens and then reports.

"Finally, 'C' talks about herself, with 'A' and 'B' listening and reporting."

★ A certain topic or issue could be assigned instead of personal introductions. This not only gives each person a chance to be heard and listened to, but allows statements and inferences to be separated and discussed with the entire group afterwards.

Training Without Fear

The next time you plan an in-house training event, form a 'training circle' from experienced employees, trainees and first-line managers. Their challenge will be to determine realistic training targets, procedures, tools and evaluation. Trainees' fear of the training program is reduced appreciably when they know that their peer group played a significant role in program selection and design. Recognizing that the program was done *for* them rather than *to* them makes the whole situation more palatable.

Could you apply this approach to an institution-based course? Could you ask your students early in the course to decide what they think ought to be included and omitted, which techniques of instruction should be used a great deal, which sparingly? Why not?

Adapted from:
Robinson, L. "Training Circles, the Fearless Way To Train." **Training and Development Journal.** July 1982. p. 12.

Find out what your participants' needs and expectations are! Either prior to planning a course or, at least, early in the event, ask them to express their needs regarding the content and the process.

Recommended to
- help learners identify their desired learning outcome
- find out which instructional techniques they are familiar with, which they prefer to learn by, which they would rather not see used
- assist the instructor in shaping a course according to the needs of the students.

Group Size
Any.

Time Required
Between two and 20 minutes, depending on the time used to discuss needs in class.

Materials Required.
Blank sheets of paper or prepared questionnaires.

Process
1. The quickest way to obtain information on learners' needs is to prepare a list of topics, issues, skills, etc. and present them to the class in the form of a questionnaire. People can then choose which they prefer, either by giving each a rating, or ranking them in order of their significance. This gives the instructor a quick feel-of-the-pulse, and allows students to choose from a menu without having to be too clear on what their specific needs are.

2. Another approach is to give each person a sheet of paper which has on it such questions as:
   - what would you like to learn during this course in terms of *skills* and information (knowledge)?
   - what kinds of activities would you prefer *not* to get involved in?
   - what kinds of activities would make this course most enjoyable for you?
   - what would SUCCESS look like for you at the end of this course (or this session)?
   - how can the instructor be most useful to you in your learning?
   - what contributions do you think you can make to the learning of others in the class?

   Collect the papers and prepare a summary of the ideas for distribution to the class. You may ask for random verbal comments along with the written questions if you wish to start off with a discussion of students' expectations.

3. A third approach would be to generate students' comments and *process* them right then and there.
   - ask participants to form sub-groups of three to five and isolate themselves from the other groups in the room.
   - issue felt pens and a sheet of newsprint to each group.
   - ask the groups to make a list of at least 10 things they want to learn during this course (this session, this term). One person is to act as recorder, but not chairperson. Tell groups that "Any contribution is OK and there is no need to reach consensus on any of the items." Set a time limit.

   Circulate through the room; keep out of the discussions except to clarify the task if groups are unsure of what to do. Leave two short strips of masking tape with each group for later use.

Next comes the *publishing* stage of the exercise. Two approaches can work for you.
★ You might ask the group to narrow their list down to the three, or five, most pressing items on the list. Allow a few minutes for this forced ranking.

You can then ask the recorder to become the reporter for the group and report to the class as a whole the recorded items. You write them down on either chalkboard or flipchart, possibly arranging them according to content, sequence or under such headings as "possible in this course", "not possible in this course", "not possible, but alternatives are available", or similar headings of your choice.

★ An *alternative* publishing technique is to ask the recorders to post their sheets along one wall of the room. Invite participants to gather around and visit the gallery, have a good look at everyone's list.

Comment on similarities and contrasts, ask for clarification on vague items, encourage people who have questions on others' entries to direct their questions to the originator, and generally have a structured yet open discussion of what the class expects.

Relate participants' needs to your expectations and needs and discuss where and how the two overlap, contradict and complement each other.

Advantages

For the learners:

Having made an attempt to identify his learning needs, the adult gets an early sense of responsibility in this course; he can now watch for problems and issues to be explored; he can see how an otherwise anonymous course becomes a personal learning project towards the satisfaction of his needs; he can hold the instructor responsible if the course develops away from the expressed needs of the learners; he can assess his own learning at the end of the course.

For the instructor:

By helping the learners to identify their needs, you have begun to demonstrate *your* definition of your role in this course—that of the facilitator of learning. You have a feel for the interests, backgrounds and needs of the learners and can begin to select strategies that are likely to help them move towards their goals. You can consider ways to individualize instruction; you have given your learners an opportunity to share with you the responsibility for the success of the course. You have begun to move your group towards becoming a learning community.

Variations

Two techniques that you can adopt to determine the expectations of your next group:

★ Post sheet(s) of newsprint that look like this:

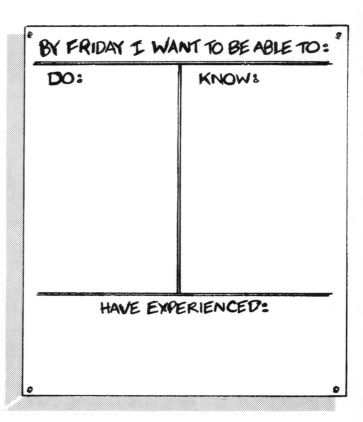

If your group consists of ten or fewer persons, ask everyone to step up to the sheet and write their ideas as key words, using boldly colored felt pens. If the group is larger, ask participants to gather their responses in small groups of three to six; a recorder then transcribes their key words onto the newsprint. It remains posted for everyone to see and for you to respond to. (These are expectations. Are they reasonable in light of your experience and the plans that you have made?).

At various points through the course you and the learners can scan the list and use it to evaluate your progress.

★ At the outset of a session, present participants with a statement of your goals and design, making clear that these do not dictate *their* goals. Involve the group in the writing of goals[1] and building of an agenda[2]. Then, using the agenda, your group is able to distinguish between content and process, sense who is controlling what, and help manage the group's time. You the trainer can learn how much of the learning process is being controlled by just one person (you) and how this shared approach can release the group's energy. An agenda sheet may look like this (use lots of color and symbols for emphasis):

AGENDA

CONTENT	WHO	PROCESS	TIME
WHAT WE'VE DONE SINCE LAST WEEK	MARY	STARTING UP	15'
GOALS & AGENDA	REG	DISCUSSION	10'
PLANNING MODELS	REG	LECTURETTE	20'
NEEDS ASSESSMENT	GEORGE	GROUP EXERCISE	60'
GROUP CRITIQUE	ALL	ROUND-THE-ROOM	12'
GOALS FOR NEXT SESSION	REG	HANDOUT	3'

The second item was submitted by Reg Herman. He suggests these for additional reading:

[1] *Robert Mager.* **Goal Analysis.** *Belmont, CA: Fearon. 1972.*

[2] *M. Doyle & D. Straus.* **How to make meetings work.** *Chicago: Playboy Press Paperback. $2.50.*

"Each individual joins the [learning] group for the purpose of satisfying some psychological need or needs. He thus brings to the group a degree of energy that he has committed to the group's activities. **Synergy** is the total of this individual energy that is available to the group. Some major portion of the group's synergy must be used to deal with interpersonal relations in the group. In any group there is a certain amount of friction resulting from status striving, power seeking, member incompatibility, etc. The portion of the group's energy that must be diverted to establish cohesion and harmony in the group is called 'maintenance synergy.' This requirement for synergy is met first, since the group would otherwise disintegrate. That which is left over (called 'effective energy') can be used to achieve the goals of the group."

Cattell, R.B. "Concepts and methods in the measurement of group syntality." **Psychological Review.** 1948, 55, 48-63.

A learning contract is a simple but explicit agreement specifying and ratifying mutual expectations between two or more persons.

Using the term "contract" suggests that you consider this agreement important, legitimate, fair and possible.

I have used contracts with individual students in a wide variety of subjects and course formats. They are based on this premise: not all people come to my courses with the same set of expectations, the same needs, the same previous experiences. I therefore feel in a quandary when I expect everyone to do the same amount of work, write the same quizzes and tests, complete the same assignments and projects and expect the same amount of reading, preparation and participation. A contract serves to recognize these differences. It also personalizes and legitimizes each participant's unique situation. I usually prepare a standard form with appropriate blank spaces, which is "negotiated, completed and signed" in class. Thus it becomes a class and a personal contract at the same time. It could contain:

- the learner's specific goals
- agreed upon steps that must be completed to reach the goal(s)
- amount of reading and out-of-class preparation
- degree and nature of class participation
- method of grading
- attendance requirements
- topic and format of individual projects.

Learners and instructor each keep a copy, which is signed and dated. If any items are subject to renegotiation, this must be indicated. As certain parts of the contract are completed or changed, this is written into the contract. At the end of the course, or at mid-stream evaluation points, the contract forms the basis for assessment and possible changes.

This strategy is probably the most important first step towards establishing an effective community of learners. It demonstrates that each student is indeed responsible for and in charge of his own learning. It specifies (or implies) the functions and responsibilities of the facilitator and those of the learners.

Caution

Making a big production might frighten students and defeat the sharing quality of contracts. Try a simple aspect of the course first, such as attendance, reading or project work.

Grading Criteria and Procedures
(for a course on Effective Interpersonal Relations)

If you do not want a "Grade" for your work in the course:
you can choose to "audit"—pay fees and attend classes, participate fully, but you will not be required to do a video tape final (non-career program students only).

You can choose to receive "credit" if your in-class performance is assessed to be at least at the "C" level (described below). You are *not* required to do a video tape final (non-career program students only).

You can expect to receive an "A" in the course if you;
are able to attend, observe accurately, listen, respond specifically, help others personalize a problem (in-class performance);
demonstrate an overall understanding of the helping model presented in this course in a written essay exam (final);
help someone personalize a problem on the video final.

You can expect to receive a "B" in the course if you:
are able to attend, observe and listen accurately, respond specifically, and "send" effectively (in-class performance);
demonstrate an overall understanding of the helping model presented in this course in a written essay exam (final);
help someone personalize a problem on the video final.

You can expect to receive a "C" in the course if you:
are able to attend, observe and listen accurately and respond specifically, to others in the class;
demonstrate an overall understanding of the helping model presented in this course in a written essay exam (final).

NOTE: any student absent for more than nine of the 45 hours of class may be asked to repeat the course.

What you can expect to gain from the course:
• Knowledge of communication and helping skills
• Ability to attend, observe, listen and respond more accurately
• Ability to express yourself more clearly and constructively
• Increased awareness of your self, feelings, thoughts.

What you can expect from the instructor:
• To model the skills and qualities being taught so you can see how they work
• To lecture clearly so the skills and the theory can be understood
• To train you (in small groups) in the use of the skills
• To be available for consultation about personal concerns related to the course outside class (not long-term counselling).

What the course expects of you:
• To attend all 45 hours (those who are absent nine hours or more may be asked to take the course over)
• To read assigned readings outside of class
• To participate verbally in small groups (and share some personal but not deep issues)
• To practice skills outside of class.

Whenever you want to generate involvement of all participants, buzz groups might be the way to go. This technique is practical with groups at any level of group experience, can be used at any stage of a course or presentation, and quickly turns one-way into two-way communication.

Recommended to
- discuss an assigned topic
- solve a problem (posed by you or the group)
- make lists of questions, comments, ideas
- relate classroom theory to the participants' own experiences.

Group Size
Any number, even large groups of one hundred and more. Each buzz group, however, is best limited to 4 to 6 persons.

Time Required
Four to six minutes for the "buzz," plus time for briefing and reporting.

Materials Required
Depending on the reporting procedure (see **Variations** below), you need newsprint, felt pens and masking tape.

Physical Setting
If chairs are movable, ask learners to move so that they can face each other. If seats are fixed, two to three people turn to the two to three people behind them to form buzz groups.

Process
1. Explain buzzing procedure and ask class to turn towards each other to form groups of four to six people. They will probably need your help to form groups the first time you ask, but the following times this will occur with little interruption or delay.
2. Clearly state the problem or issue; write it on the board, flipchart or overhead transparency.
3. Inform groups of time limit (four to six minutes).
4. Suggest groups select recorder/spokesperson.
5. Perhaps suggest ways to approach the problem.
6. Float from group to group to assist them in getting started, keeping on topic and within the guidelines you have suggested. It is vital that this occurs, or else groups tend to drift off the task and miss out on the value of the exercise.
7. Inform class of "two minutes remaining." At this stage a shortening or lengthening of time may seem appropriate. Decide and inform the groups.
8. Call time, "even if you haven't quite finished."
9. Request a brief report from one spokesperson per group. To avoid duplication/repetition ask each succeeding speaker only to add points that have not been raised. Use different spokespeople every time you use this technique.
10. Process the material generated by the groups. This may mean that you incorporate it in the lecture that follows, that you assign a new topic for discussion, or ?? In any case, reinforce the efforts and comments from the group so that you get equal or even more contributions the next time you ask learners to "form buzz groups, please."

Variations
- Not all buzz groups need to report, only those who have new information to contribute. This avoids time-consuming repetition and the individuals becoming bored.

- in a large class, have each spokesperson report only their main point. This avoids having the first group report the bulk of the information with others not being able to contribute.
- buzz groups summarize or point-list their findings on a large piece of newsprint/posterpaper. All sheets are posted next to each other and the group reads, asks, reflects, discusses and adds.

Best Used

- in conjunction with lecture.
  Before: to determine the learners' previous knowledge, their expectations, their problem areas.
  During: to see if the class is with you, if you are being understood before going on to a new concept.
  After: to help integrate new information/concepts with previous learning, to identify problem areas for further discussion/explanation, to receive feedback on your presentation.
- as a warm-up activity. Participants could be asked to form sub-groups, introduce themselves and determine one or two specific expectations they share. A list of these expectations could then form the basis for an all-class discussion on what the course will and will not be about. Students are immediately involved without being put on the spot in front of an entire group of strangers.
- as an evaluation tool at points throughout or at the end of the course. While individuals might be reluctant to offer honest criticism of the course and in-structor, they usually find it easier to do so as part of a group. Spokespersons too are more at ease in reporting comments regarding their instructor if they speak on behalf of their group.

An Israeli study showed that students who were told jokes at the beginning of lectures fared 22% better on exams than their colleagues in drearier classrooms.

The New Yorker, *December 6, 1982, p. 40.*

Most adult students expect to be lectured to. They come with note pads and pens and are prepared to sit through what are often boring lectures. Many instructors, too, dread the boring-lecture-monster and wish there were ways to prevent it from rearing its ugly head. Some time ago an experiment was conducted in California: a college course was taught by both regular professors and professional actors who had been carefully briefed in the subject. The students did not know about this experiment. At the end of the term the examination results were compared and the overwhelming evidence was (you guessed it) those instructed by actors had acquired more information (i.e. learned more) than those taught by the subject experts. Do we need to take acting lessons?

Recommended When

- you are concerned mainly with giving information
- the information is not readily available in another form
- the material is needed for short-term retention only
- you are introducing a subject or giving oral directions that will lead to other techniques which involve the learner actively.

Not Recommended When

- the material is complex, abstract or very detailed
- you are dealing with learning that involves the attitudes and feelings of your learners
- the information must be available in its fullest form for long-term retention
- you are working with a group of learners whose level of educational experience is minimal
- the learner is required to integrate the material with previous learning or back-home experiences.

Group Size
Any.

Time Required
Unless an instructor is very entertaining, the subject matter most compelling and the audience superbly committed, experience suggests that a lecture should last no longer than 30 minutes. In other words, try to limit your straight lecturing to between 20 and 30 minutes. At that point utilize an instructional technique that requires the learner to change from passive to active behavior, from listening to doing, from you doing most of the work to the student doing most of it.

There is no reason why you could not have a one or even two-hour lecture, as long as you mix up the techniques . . . and keep your learners involved.

Materials Required
None for the lecture, unless you think visual aids would help you make the point better.

Physical Setting
Each student should have a full view of the lecturer at all times.

Effective Lecturing: A Few Tricks of the Trade
- Do not present too many points. Six major points are probably enough for half an hour
- Present summaries both at the beginning and the end
- Pause occasionally to give listeners a chance to catch up and summarize for themselves
- Make it clear when and how questions will be dealt with. Some choices are: "Keep your questions until the end of the first twenty minutes. I shall then pause and make sure your questions are heard." Or: "Let me just finish this diagram and then we'll take a few moments to deal with your questions. Please hang on until then."

Or: "I'd prefer to present my lecture in its entirety and then deal with questions. Just to make sure yours aren't lost, I suggest that any time you have a question you jot it down. Chances are they will be answered as I proceed. If not, raise yours at the end."

- If you say you will deal with questions, allow time for them!
- Use visual aids to support your points. Some specific techniques are explained on pages 85-87.
- Your rate of speaking and choice of vocabulary should be appropriate to the level of comprehension of your group. Build 'in checks to see if everybody understands the points you are making. (**Spend-a-penny** and **Speedy Memo** are just two techniques you can employ in conjunction with your lectures to give you such a check)
- Even with the use of visual aids, a lecture essentially remains a one-way communication method.

Variations

★ A "lecturette" is a short lecture lasting not more than 10 minutes. A complex lecture can be broken up into several lecturettes, allowing you to incorporate other techniques. A lecturette requires discipline and organization from you, tends to put fewer people to sleep and increases your chances of success.

If this approach appeals to you, but you aren't sure that you can stick to the 10-minute intervals, try something that worked for me. I set a kitchen timer at the 10-minute mark and placed it in full view for all to see. I explained what I was attempting to do and everybody in the room became part of my experiment. (That's *one* way to get your students' attention . . .).

★ A "lecture-forum" involves interrupting a longish lecture with a brief question-and-answer period. It provides activity for the learners by asking them to examine a portion of the lecture in detail before more information is presented. Be alert to avoid being led astray. Rather than asking: "Are there any questions?" you might start with: "How could you apply the 3 points I have just discussed in your own work situations?" Or: "What additional information do you need to understand this important step in the process?" As soon as you are satisfied that the group is with you, proceed.

★ "Fill in the blanks[1]" is a useful way to assist learners in note-taking and ensure that they focus on your main points. As you make your important points, participants can fill in the blanks on the handout you have prepared. They learn by seeing and hearing as you speak, but also by repeating in writing. An example of such a handout appears on page 39.

A Few Extra Pointers

- Mix your activities in such a way that the students are alternately passive (sit, hear, see) and active (problem-solve, write, construct, discuss, move, walk, speak, operate equipment).
- Introduce your topic by specifying what will be presented, how long it will take, and how you are going to proceed with it. This helps learners anticipate events, prepare for change in pace/technique and assign their energy accordingly.
- Present new material in a logical sequence, step by step, relating it to familiar and known material (such as readings, previous discussions, student's own experience).
- Allow extra time for complex material and repeat key points.
- Consider giving handouts either before or after presentation.

Use special cues to keep your audience interested. Try to . . .

- **change place**: move around, speak from the back of the room, the front, the left or the right of the room. I have been known to stand on top of a table to make a point.
- **use gestures**: hand, head and body movements can serve as supporters (and distractors!) of verbal output.
- **concentrate attention**: "Now listen to carefully!!!", or, "Look at this graph. . . ."
- **vary style of interaction**: use questions, student-student interactions, buzz-groups, demonstrations, problem-solving, tasks, discussions.
- **use silence**: for reflection, question formulation, concentration.
- **change tone of voice**: loud-mellow, fast-slow, happy-sad, technical-personal, etc.
- **experiment!**

When I switch to techniques other than lecturing, I become less tied to my notes and my spot in front of the class. I discover each time, that I have more time and energy to spend on helping my students learn. Instead of saying "Oops, there goes the time, quickly two more points and then I'll see you next time," I can be more available to my students.

The most important service I can provide to participants is to assist them to take charge of their own learning. Cutting down on lectures and providing instead carefully structured activities always permits me to do just that. I suggest you experiment with new ideas only at a pace that is comfortable for you. Arrange for your students to share the responsibility for the success of the course.

FILL IN THE BLANKS

Topic: Managing Conflict

Principles: Costs:

    1. Conflict is_____. _____

    2. Conflict can be desirable when it is_____.

    3. Uncontrolled conflict is

    _____. _____

Controlled Conflict:

    1. Deal with conflict_____.

    2. Identify the_____problem.

    3. Handle _____.

    4. Consider the_____traits involved.

    5. Ask for_____and proposed solutions.

    6. Avoid_____, use logic.

    7. Think it_____.

    8. Schedule a_____session.

[1]Contributed by Susan Reuthe, Training Director, Charles Schwab & Co. San Francisco, CA.

The Inquiry Method

Neil Postman and Charles Weingartner say that the attitudes and beliefs of the instructor are "the air of a learning environment"; they determine the quality of life within. Since these attitudes are reflected in the behavior of the teacher, Postman and Weingartner describe their "inquiry teacher" as a person who:

. . . rarely tells students what he thinks they ought to know. He believes that telling, if it is the major way of instructing, deprives the learner of the excitement and opportunity of self-directed and powerful learning.

. . . uses questioning as his major mode of interacting. Rather than trying to seduce students into reciting what he (or some other authority) considers the right answers, he sees questions as instruments to open minds to unexpected possibilities.

. . . generally does not accept a single statement as an answer to a question, not because he does not like right answers, but because too often the "right answer" only serves to discourage further thought.

. . . encourages student-student interaction as opposed to teacher-student interaction. He thus tries to minimize his role as the sole arbiter of what is acceptable and what is not.

. . . rarely sums up the position taken by students. He sees learning as a process, not a finished product and fears that his "closures" might have the effect of ending further thought.

. . . measures his success in terms of behavioral changes in his learners. He does so by observing the frequency with which they ask questions; the increase in relevance of their questions; the frequency and conviction of their challenges to statements by other learners, the teacher or the text; their willingness to modify their positions when new data warrants such changes; the increase in their skills in observing, classifying, generalizing and their ability to apply the latter to situations in an original way.

Postman, N. and Weingartner, C. **Teaching as a Subversive Activity.** *New York: Delta Books. 1969. p 25-37.*

This technique is useful when you want to get quick input from each participant, but don't want to go into a small group activity.

Recommended To
- get a quick statement about an issue from each person in the group
- require all persons in the group to listen while only one speaks
- demonstrate to the class that the instructor values the contributions of all members of the group
- give participants an opportunity to become involved, even if normally they would keep in the background.

Group Size
Best if there are less than 20 participants. If the class is larger, two people could work together and contribute one joint statement.

Time Required
Between 10 and 30 seconds per person.

Materials
Nothing special is required.

Physical Setting
Ask participants to take their chairs and form a circle. If that is not possible, people should at least be able to face each other while speaking.
If the seating is fixed, ask everybody to turn so that they can see the speaker as everyone has a turn.

Process
1. Arrange seating as described above. Everybody should be able to see and hear all members of the group. If this is a new thing for your participants, be clear and firm with the instructions.
2. State a question or issue on which each person in the class is briefly to give their position/feeling/opinions. The questions or issues may have been raised by students or the instructor.
3. Explain that each person will be asked to respond and that no interruptions/comments will be allowed while a person speaks.
4. Ask the person on your left to start, then ask each person in turn, until everyone has had an opportunity to respond. Start with a different person each time you use this technique.
5. Encourage each speaker (especially the shy ones) by displaying your interest: nod, smile, have eye contact with the speaker. You may want to ask a clarifying question ("What I hear you say is...is that correct?") but do not evaluate or criticize contributions. Your "modeling" behavior is likely to set the mood of the circle response.
6. Enforce the one-statement-per-person rule and stop those who want to digress.
7. After the last person has responded, thank participants for their contributions, and summarize the contributions if you find that useful.
8. Build on the contributions in the ensuing session.
9. You may find it helpful to explore with the group the possible advantages of this technique. Ask if it should be done again; if so, does anybody suggest any alterations?

Teaching Adult Learners On Their Own Terms

Needs, goals, objectives. Programs for adult learners need to be attuned both to social priorities and to those needs that are perceived by the learner rather than those perceived by the educator. Individuals enter the educational process with their unique needs, motives and objectives, and seek to satisfy them by selecting programs from a variety of sources.

Content. Adults typically enter into further education to seek help in dealing with life problems rather than to master a body of knowledge for its own sake. Some will be looking for information only, while others will be there to gain expertise in various intellectual skills, motor skills, and attitudes that have immediate application to their life situation. Content selection should be flexible to ensure that these learners' needs are met, not those of the designer.

Learning Environment. It may be the traditional classroom, or the home, the place of employment, the community-at-large, or other places not traditionally connected to formal learning. Each setting makes different demands on the educational planner.

Instructional Strategy. Adults typically want to experience in success, select content of interest to them, participate when they are ready, attend when they can, leave when they want or when their needs have been met, and return when they desire to learn more.

Program objectives should be presented explicitly so that adults can choose a certain program or search further for an alternative. Material should be selected to built on adults' existing experiences and to stress current needs. Ample opportunity should be provided to practise new skills in the right setting. Feedback should be provided to permit learners to assess their progress.

Evaluation. Adults demand to be involved in evaluation jointly with the institution. Adults are the ones who will decide whether a program was of value.

Adapted from:
Gary Hull & Vincent De Sanctis. **Audiovisual Instruction.** Nov. 1979. pp. 14-15.

This is a technique which can be used at various points in a session and will give everyone the chance to get involved in the topic under exploration. It requires no previous practice and can be interjected without much trouble.

Recommended To
- review previously presented information
- concentrate the group's energy on one problem, issue or question
- allow each person to be part of a team effort
- allow each person to become actively involved in the teaching/learning process without
  (a) being put on the spot
  (b) becoming bored
  (c) having to fight for air-time.

Group Size
Any size over 12; if less use **Circle Response.**

Time Required
Between eight and twenty minutes, depending on the group's experience with this method and the type of problem.

Physical Setting
Room for a small group to sit in a circle.

Process
1. Ask your class to form working groups of about five persons each and disperse throughout the room so that each team has some privacy.
2. Ask each group to designate a recorder, who will not act as a chairperson, but merely record the group's response to the problem. The recorder may be appointed, elected or people may take turns.
3. Clarify the question to which groups are to respond. (Such question may result from events in the classroom [process] or may relate to the course topic [content].)
4. Make sure everyone understands the question and the way in which the groups are to operate. Avoid questions that can be answered with a Yes or a No.
5. Using the same pattern and rules as explained under **Circle Response**, each group proceeds. Start with one person designated by you: "Let's start with the people who are sitting on the window side of the room, and go clockwise." (This part goes more smoothly once the class has some experience in working in groups.) In any case, a quick review of the simple rules might be useful:
   - No member may skip his turn
   - No member may contribute until the person next to him has finished
   - No one may answer on behalf of someone else or criticize a contribution.
6. The recorder is the only one writing, simply listing the contribution of each participant in the circle. Suggest to him that a phrase or key point would be enough for each response.
7. At the end of the predetermined time call "stop" and ask people in their circles turn slightly so that the whole class can now begin sharing their suggestions.
8. Repeat the questions again and ask a representative from each sub-group in turn to read one of the responses given by his group.
9. You may want to write down key words of the answers on the board or a flip chart. Ask the group recorders to check their lists and cross out the words that are similar/identical to the one just put up.
10. Follow this procedure until all of the contributions have been "published."

Seating Arrangements Influence Group Interaction

Researchers have analyzed the interaction process of groups seated at round tables and found that group members sitting across from each other followed one another in speaking more often than they followed persons in other positions[1]. A similar result was obtained by using rectangular tables. Persons sitting at the ends of the table participated more than others in the group. The possibility of having eye contact with group members tends to increase interaction, regardless of relative seating distance.

Reported in: Shaw, M.E. **Group Dynamics**. New York: McGraw-Hill. 1976. pp 148-151

This is a simple but effective technique to stimulate equal participation in the course activities by all members. It can be quickly inserted into any learning activity.

Recommended To
- make contributing a fun exercise
- emphasize that each person has equal rights and obligations to the class and themselves
- compel frequent contributors to save their comments and allow others to speak.

Group Size
Any.

Time Required
Enough time to explain the rules and distribute pennies. The rest fits into whatever activity your class happens to be involved in.

Material
Three pennies (or tokens) per person.

Physical Setting
Participants remain in their seats.

Process
1. People stay in their normal seats.
2. Everyone is given three pennies.
3. Pennies can be spent during the following class session at the discretion of each person: "Every time you speak in class, you'll have to spend one of your pennies by putting it in front of you. Once your pennies are spent, you have to wait and be quiet (until the next issue). Everybody has equal opportunities."
4. You now proceed with your discussion, lecture, demonstration or whatever.

Effective For
- dealing with the "expert" in the class who always has something to say and probably intimidates other, less vocal members. Frequent contributors often respond in two ways:
1) "For once, I could sit back and let the others speak. I always felt obligated to contribute because I have had some previous experience. . . ."
2) "Gee, it wasn't easy to sit back and watch my pennies. Speaking comes so easily to me and I never really knew that some of these people had so much to say."
- encouraging shy students. Participants who normally would not participate have told me with amazement that they too had spent a penny or two: "I didn't think I would, but suddenly it was so easy to speak up."
- a discussion at the end of the class could be used to find out how different people felt about the exercise. After you have used it a few times with the same class there will be no need for the pennies. A cooperative spirit will likely prevail.

Use Brainstorming to Break the Ice and Solve a Problem

Brainstorming can be used in many ways for a number of goals. Here is an example in which it was used as an ice breaker with a new group, and as a way to identify certain problems. The trainer's task was to introduce a new registration form to a group of government employees. For many this could seem like a dull topic, and a threatening one if you were being asked to give up a beloved old form for an unknown new one.

The trainer "warmed" the group to the topic and each other by asking them to brainstorm on the range of problems the new form was likely to present. After ten minutes of this, everyone in the class had had a chance to speak, even those who would otherwise have been silent. Then he distributed the new form, and explained its features. Next, the group again looked at the flipchart listing potential problem areas and, with the help of the trainer, was able to see how these were dealt with on the new form. Their acceptance of the new form was thus greatly enhanced.

Contributed by:
Sean Gregg, Employment Counsellor, Employment & Immigration Canada

This is just the thing when you want to draw on the group's collective creative energy. It permits uninhibited participation by each person and often results in surprising ideas and new solutions to old problems.

Recommended To
- deal with problems relating to course content
- deal with problems arising from the process occuring in the classroom.
- generate a multitude of ideas by drawing on every participant's creativity.

Group Size
Any size, as long as it can be divided into groups of not more than about eight people.

Time Required
Until group "exhausts" and no further ideas are forthcoming; about 5 to 15 minutes plus time for discussion.

Physical Setting
All participants face a chalkboard or flip-chart where the recorder(s) write down the ideas generated by the group.

Process
1. Display problem so that everyone can read it. Examples: "How can a manager avoid wasting time with telephone calls?" Or: "How can we make it possible for everyone to participate equally in class discussions?"
2. Decide to divide into sub-groups of about five to eight people each, or work with the entire class.
3. Give the following instructions (write them on the board in point form):
   - during the next 8 minutes you are to come up with as many ideas as you can on how to solve the problem. The emphasis is on quantity. Try to generate as many ideas as quickly as you can.
   - any idea is allowed, there are no dumb or impossible ideas at this stage.
   - the crazier the better.
   - try to piggy-back: for example, if someone's idea reminds you of another, say it, even if it sounds similar.
   - no criticism is allowed. We will evaluate the ideas later.
4. Designate one or two people to be the recorders so that contributions can be written down as they appear. The visual display of ideas often sparks others.
5. Call time when the announced time is almost up, or when you feel the group has exhausted the fund of ideas.
6. Tell your group: "Now review the list of ideas and identify the three solutions you feel are most useful. You have about three to five minutes." (Or you can lead this step yourself.)
7. Reconvene and have sub-groups report their solutions, writing them up (or hanging their sheets of paper next to each other).
8. Finally, have the whole group (including yourself as consultant) decide which ideas are useful. In the case of a problem related to the in-class process this would also mean: "Which solution(s) do we want to implement in this class?"

Here is a quick way to see what everybody is thinking about what's going on in the room—without a lengthy discussion and without anyone being left out. A good technique for mid-stream evaluation of process, as well as a nice way to get everyone's opinion on this or that.

Recommended To
- get almost instant feedback from a group of students on their feelings, thoughts or attitudes
- ensure that the instructor can respond to moods and reactions in the class without lengthy discussions and without anybody being put on the spot.

Group Size
Any.

Time Required
Less than a coffee break.

Physical Setting
The existing one.

Process
1. Ask your students to sit back for a moment; explain what you want to know. Examples: 'What do you think of today's session?' 'How would you describe your feelings about this class right now?' 'What is your opinion of the material I have presented so far?' 'How well am I able to help you learn this material?' (Of course, you'd only ask one of these questions at a time).
2. Make sure each person has a piece of paper.
3. Request that each person write just one word on it in answer to your question. Ask for a noun, an adjective, a verb or an exclamation.
4. Quickly collect the papers, mix them up, and ask one or two people to read them out loud. This allows everyone

to know what the class members are thinking and feeling.
5. Respond to the message the group is giving you!

Case in Point
Once I thought I had presented a bomb; that my lecture had not been very good and the students had gone home unhappy. I felt disturbed. The next morning, before we did anything else, I asked them all to describe in one word how they remembered the last session. The responses had a multiple effect:
a) I was told that my presentation had been exciting and thought-provoking. People had left the room in a rather thoughtful mood not because of a job poorly done, but because of one done well.
b) The students responded with amazement to the fact that I had thought about them and they treated me with considerable care and gentleness after that.

On another occasion, in the middle of a one-day workshop, I wanted to know how we were progressing. Should we continue at the pace we had all morning or slow down? I did not want to ask for fear that the more vocal students would speak "on behalf of" the quiet ones and I knew that this would not give me the true picture. A speedy memo helped answer my questions.

Nine Tips for Effective Instruction

Gagne[1] describes effective instructional situations and identifies nine components that ought to be present in such events. The sequence is not important, but try to include as many of them as possible in your classroom learning events:

•Gain and control attention

Advertising people seem to have a knack for this, as do some entertainers and lecturers. Use gestures, announcements or displays to direct the learners' attention to what is to be learned.

•Inform the learners of the expected outcome

"Here's what you can expect to gain from listening to me" (or participating, experimenting, studying).

•Stimulate recall of relevant pre-requisites

"Remember the last time you tried to get your boss to listen to you, but ended up frustrated and angry?" Or, "Last week we had to interrupt our discussion at the point where two issues had emerged."

•Present new material

Here it is. Use any of the strategies in this book, plus many more that you can come up with yourself.

•Offer guidance for learning

"Let me give you an example from my own time as a desk clerk." Or, "I wonder if you, John, could tell us how useful this new system could be in your company." Or, "I have prepared a few problems I'd like you to try and solve right now. Use the formula on the board as much as possible." Or, "What kind of problems does this new information give you?"

•Provide feedback

Inform the learners (or create situations that will), of the "correctness" of responses, answers and solutions.

•Appraise the performance

Before moving to the next set of new ideas, the learners ought to have a chance to assess themselves against some kind of external standard (model, test, examination, real-life, try-out).

•Make transferability possible

Adults learn not for the instructor's sake, but in order to improve their job performance, their academic knowledge, their hobby skills, their functioning as a parent, or their enjoyment of life in general. Through such strategies as role-play, shop/laboratory practice, and simulated events, the learners may practice the application of new learning right in the classroom. If that is difficult to achieve, assignments can be given and reports brought back (during the next session) which provide for an assessment and transfer of that learning to the outside world.

•Ensure retention

Once learning has taken place, it should be incorporated into further study; new information related to old, problems solved by using the new learning, and application made through repeated questions, puzzles, and other methods.

---

[1]Gagne, R.M. **The Conditions of Learning**. *New York: Holt-Reinhard-Winston.*

Often a "class discussion" is little more than an opportunity for the instructor to make little speeches. If you want to turn your discussions into occasions where *everyone* has a chance to be heard, the following might provide you with a practical tip or two.

Recommended To
- tap the creative resources of all class members
- explore applications of theoretical course content
- obtain feedback on degree of understanding of a topic
- help students to present and defend their ideas before a group
- break up a long training session (by providing a certain entertainment value which may also act as a stimulant for further sessions).

Group Size
Ten to 15 seems ideal. If the class is larger try sub-groups or buzz groups.

Time Required
Five minutes to an hour, or until the task is accomplished.

Physical Setting
Participants should be able to see and hear each other easily; chairs arranged in a circle or around a large table, or several tables set up in a horseshoe pattern, works best.

Process
1. Assist the class in determining the topic for discussion or assign it in advance. Give specific guidelines for preparation so that participants share equal responsibility for the usefulness of discussion time. This "contracted" preparation goes a long way towards avoiding bull-sessions.
2. Arrange physical setting. Encourage people to change from their usual seating into whatever arrangement you consider useful: "Please bring your chairs around in a circle for our discussion," and "Would you move in a bit so that we can all see each other?"
3. Have a few starter questions or statements prepared to get things rolling in the direction you want them to go. Much depends on your time constraints and the degree to which you want people to really explore *their* approaches to the topic. Can you allow the group to digress a bit? When do you cut in and gently bring them back on topic? How much can you allow one or two group members to dominate the discussion? Decide these questions for yourself in advance of the discussion so that you can be consistent in class.
4. At the outset, clarify the *objective* of the discussion (what you expect to be the end result of the exercise), the *process* you wish the group to adopt (how the discussion ought to proceed, which rules should be followed), and what your role will be.
5. Encourage silent members to participate: "Fred, you mentioned earlier that.... How could that fit in here?" Or: "Maggie, is this a situation you can help us with?"
6. Dominant members (or those who find it easy to speak up on this or any other topic) often have a need to show their experience and knowledge to the group. Your task is to encourage and channel that energy. You could ask such persons to:
   - prepare a position statement in advance of the discussion, as a starter
   - assist the class by acting as discussion-leader in a sub-group
   - act as observer and thus help the group sharpen its discussion skills (and their own sensitivity to the contribution of others).
7. Be prepared to clarify things when

the discussion becomes muddled or confused. Be careful not to sneak in your own bias!

8. A summary can be useful, but is not necessary. Sometimes a group leaves a topic unresolved, people think about it and may bring it up later. If it is possible and appears useful, you may ask one or two students to sum up the outcome of the discussion. Or, go around the group at the end and ask each person for a one-sentence summary.

Content and Process

One important distinction that can be made when observing group discussion is that of content versus process. When you consider what your group is discussing, you are referring to *content*. When you look at such issues as who speaks to whom, or what types of behavior occur in your groups, you are observing *process*. Many novice groups have difficulties with process (which may translate into difficulties regarding content) and you may wish to help. The first aspect of group process you might observe is the pattern of communication[1]:

★ Who talks? For how long? How often?

★ Whom do people look at when they talk:
  a) individuals
  b) the group
  c) nobody

★ Who talks after whom, or who interrupts whom?

The next time your class has a discussion, keep out of the way and observe. You might also invite others to act in the observer's role, as long as you all report back to the group what you have observed. Groups often get so wrapped up in working on content that process is ignored. Just receiving feedback on it and being invited to suggest changes can be a powerful remedy to discussion problems.

Discussions appear informal and easy to use. Sometimes instructors use them without giving much thought to their planning and execution. However, for a discussion to be useful learning strategy it must be carefully timed, prepared, structured, observed and concluded.

Task, Maintenance and Self-Oriented Behavior

If you plan to use a great deal of group discussion in your course, it may be worth your while to spend some energy helping your learners learn by this method. Researchers of group dynamics suggest that behavior in groups can be viewed in terms of what its purpose or function seems to be. A person saying something that has to do directly with the content and purpose of the discussion is said to display *task behavior*. Another trying to involve a silent neighbor in the discussion is engaged in *maintenance behavior*, and yet another meeting personal needs without consideration for the group's concern is exhibiting *self-oriented behavior*. As the group becomes more experienced in the use of the discussion technique, more of the behavior will be in the first two categories and less in the last. Giving your group feedback on their behavior, or better, encouraging members to become self-observers, will help this process along.

Here are more details on the three types of group behavior[2]. They are written so that you could give them as a handout to students.

Maintenance Behaviors

Encouraging—
    Being warm and responsive to others; accepting the contributions of others; giving others an opportunity for recognition.

Expressing group feelings—
    Sensing feeling, mood, relationships within the group and sharing own feelings with other members.

Harmonizing—
    Attempting to reconcile differences and reduce tension by giving people a chance to explore their differences.

Compromising—
    When your own idea or status is involved in a conflict, offering to compromise, admitting error, disciplining yourself to maintain group cohesion.

Gate-keeping—
    Keeping the channels of communication open and making it easy for others to participate.

Task Behaviors

Initiating-
    Proposing tasks or goals; defining group problems, suggesting a procedure or idea.

Information or opinion seeking-
    Requesting facts; asking for suggestions or ideas.

Information or opinion giving-
    Offering facts; stating beliefs; giving suggestions or ideas.

Clarifying or elaborating-
    Interpreting or restating ideas and suggestions; clearing up confusion; indicating alternatives before the group; giving examples.

Summarizing-
    Pulling together related ideas; restating suggestions after the group has discussed them; offering a decision for the group to accept or reject.

Consensus-seeking-
    Checking with the group to see how much agreement has been reached, or can possibly be reached.

Finally, there is a list of "self-serving" actions which could be used to identify possible interaction problems. As with all personal feedback that can strike a touchy spot with some individuals, it's a good idea to discuss all helpful and hindering behavior early in a group's life, before anyone gets "stuck" in a certain type of behavior.

Self-Serving Behaviors

Blocking-
    Interfering with the process of the group by rejecting ideas, taking a negative stance on all suggestions; arguing unduly; being pessimistic; refusing to cooperate.

Deserting-
    Withdrawing in some way; being indifferent, aloof, excessively formal; daydreaming; doodling; whispering to others; wandering off the subject.

Being aggressive-
    Struggling for status, boasting, criticizing, deflating ego or status of others.

Recognition seeking-
    Attempting to get attention by boasting, or claiming long experience or great accomplishments.

Talking about the practice of helpful group behavior is one thing, doing it another. On the next page is a handy form that I have used to have participants "contract" with others in the group. Use it as is or make up one that suits your situation.

References and Notes:

1) Kolb, David, et al. **Organizational Psychology—An experiential approach.** Second edition. Englewood Cliffs: Prentice Hall. 1974.

2) Many similar lists are in circulation and I was unable to determine the exact source of this one. The categories were first mentioned in: Benne, K.D. and Sheats, P. "Functional roles of group members." **Journal of Social Issues,** 2, (1948), 42-47.

Personal Action Statement
Part I

I plan to practise during this morning's session at least one of the Maintenance and one of the Task behaviors, in addition to what I do normally.

I have selected a behavior from each group which I think I may have occasional difficulty with.

My selected MAINTENANCE behavior is_____which for me will involve such helpful actions as_____
_____ .

My selected TASK behavior is_____and I plan to practise the following helpful actions_____
_____ .

To assist me in my undertaking, I will share my intentions with another person in this room:

_____(insert his/her name)

We will share our plans with each other at the outset of the discussion, agree to keep an eye on each other throughout the session, and spend a few moments before noon exchanging our observations.

Agreed: _____   _____

Part II
to be completed prior to leaving the room

As a result of the feedback I have received from my partner in this action statement, I plan to do the following (one specific task):

a) during the week_____
_____ .

b) during the next session_____
_____ .

This is a simple variation of the traditional case study method. A mini-event is described by the instructor and students discuss it in light of other materials presented.

Recommended To
- relate theory to practice and vice versa.
- analyze real life situations in light of course material.

Group Size
Any size; you may ask people to work in buzz groups.

Time Required
A snappy five minutes or a more detailed 30. If participants know about the incident in advance they can come prepared.

Process
1. Introduce the incident at the *beginning* (a warm-up for what is to come), *middle* (let's see how it fits) or *end* (so now you have the information, how would you apply it?).
2. Ask learners for their responses to specific questions. You might also want to ask them to prepare questions they need to ask before they can respond to the incident.
3. Combine the discussion with a role-play or a debate/forum if that seems useful.

Caution: *critical incidents have to be plausible to the learners. If the example is too far removed from their experience, it may be difficult to get meaningful reactions.*

Cases in Point
- The instructor has just presented a lecturette on the early indicators of "burnout" as it may occur in both work and private life. To relate the topic to the experience of the audience (a group of data processing managers) she gives them a brief scenario of "one day in the life of a programmer." The participants are asked to identify symptoms and possible causes of impending burnout in this individual's life.
- The trainer, working with a group of hotel employees, wants to dramatize the importance of emergency procedures for hospitality operations. He has rehearsed a little "game" with an outsider who is to come into the room and shout: "We've just received a bomb threat!" Reminding the class that this is a make-believe situation, he asks them each to write down two things they would do immediately if this were the real thing. Subsequent discussion might reveal a variety of approaches to the same situation and be a smart lead-in to "the *right* procedure to follow in case of a bomb threat."

Questions can be used as effective instructional tools—without embarrassing participants who don't have the 'right' answer, without students guessing what you want them to say, without the awkward pauses that occasionally set in when you say "Are there any questions?"

Try These:

Ask for more information by requiring the responder to be more explicit and perhaps more sure of his answer; "Can you give me an example?" Or, "When you say xyz, what do you mean?"

Restate what you have heard: "So, are you saying that people should . . . or did I misunderstand you?" By stating what your understanding is to this point (rather than "Would you say that again?") you provide the other with a point from which to proceed. She may respond, "No that's not what I meant. What I *am* trying to say is that. . . ."

Make critical observations to make learners look at their answer in a more probing and critical way: "To me that sounds like a rather simple answer." Or: "Why do you think this is so?" Or: "How would you explain your answer to someone who feels quite the opposite?"

Try to **intensify the learner's statement** if the response is important, requires no instructor comment, and could be added to by others. You could say: "Very good, Colin. What implications would your statement have for . . .?" (turning to the whole group). Or: "How can we use Colin's solution to solve our dilemma?"

More Tricks to Stimulate Participation:

- Ask a question, pause for five seconds and then ask for a response. Often students give non-verbal hints that they are ready to respond.
- React to "false" answers with acceptance, even if you do not agree with them. Use probing questions to refocus on the discussion topic.
- Encourage silent members to comment if you think they might have the answer but are reluctant to speak up: "This is probably something you know quite a bit about, David . . ."
- Ask the same question of several students. Don't stop after the first response, which often comes from the same core group of participants.
- Formulate questions that cause people to give long answers. Do this by (a) referring to areas of knowledge, rather than simple facts, and (b) making it difficult to answer with a simple YES or NO.
- Piggy-back your new questions on top of the responses you got for your previous question: "OK, let's take that approach and take it one step further . . ."
- Pick out certain aspects of the response and refocus the group's attention on them.
- Try not to answer your own questions too often. After a while you will be performing a one-man show.
- Avoid questions to which the answer is obvious: "Don't you agree that . . .?" Make a statement instead ("I believe that . . .") and invite reactions.
- Taking that last suggestion one step further, if you ask a question, be prepared to hear the answer even if it does not coincide with your own. Be flexible.

When Did You Last Ask, "Are There Any Questions?"

You can probably remember the silence that often follows this question. Some instructors use this line one minute before the class time is up (and after they have spoken for one solid hour). Would you bring up a point that you missed half way through the lecture if you were a student? Would you expect full consideration of your questions when you knew that any minute the group would get up and leave? If the instructor really wants to hear "any questions," then he must allow for time and create an atmosphere which makes it OK for people to ask. Here are some openers that can yield responses:

"Before I go on, does this make any sense to you?"

"How are we doing?"

"Where did I lose you?"

"Do my examples make sense to you?

"What additional information do you want from me?"

You have probably seen the following technique used by someone experienced in political meetings: "Are there any questions you want me to answer?" Five second pause, and then, addressing a person who either has, or ought to have, a question: "Perhaps you could start, Eileen?"

Also watch for non-verbal signals, "You seem puzzled, Eckart. Can I help?" Having the instructor accept responsibility for "helping you to understand me" makes it easier for participants to ask for clarification and additional information.

Buzz groups and **Speedy Memo** are additional ways to get around the "are there any questions?" silence.

Here is a technique in which you present a controlled, partial replication of the actual world, ask students to assume parts and then work their way through an open-ended "script." You stop the action and guide students through an analysis of the "play."

Recommended To
- provide opportunities to rehearse new behavior in a relatively safe environment.
- assist students in developing such interpersonal skills as problem-solving, counselling, interviewing.
- let students play roles that are different from their usual behavior.
- inject a 'slice of life' into the classroom

Group Size
You need your players; all others are designated as observers. There is really no limit to the size of the audience, but the larger the audience, the more you have to structure the discussion following the role-play.

Time Required
Can be as short as ten, or as long as thirty minutes. Preparation is needed in any case, depending on the complexity of the scenario and the detail in which you deal with the steps that are described below.

Physical Setting
Everyone must be able to see and hear the role-players. The play itself may require some set-up, such as an interviewer's office with desk and chairs.

Process
There are four distinct steps in a well run role play: scene-setting, role-play, debriefing, and closure.

1. Setting the Scene
Your task is to prepare the group for the role-play and provide a valid reason for its use. Several strategies are available:

- You can start with a *discussion* during which you post a number of problem situations elicited from the group. During a discussion leadership class, for instance, you might pose the question: "What do you see as the most common mistake a chairperson can make when opening a meeting?" From the discussion a list of typical errors is generated. You then suggest that one way to get a feel for the difficult task of opening a meeting would be for the group to engage in a short role-play, where one person acts as the leader and others as participants.
- You can give a *lecturette* (a prepared speech lasting no longer than 15 or 20 minutes). You could present research findings of "common meeting mistakes," with special focus on the role of the manager during the opening phase of a meeting. "Here are some of the problems you will have to deal with as effective group leaders. Now let's do a short role-play to see how it feels being a chairperson and a participant in such a situation."
- You can show a *film* of a group struggling through a meeting, and stop the film at a point where they start spinning their collective wheels.
- You can give students a *written case* which outlines a situation such as described above.

2. Role-Play
Be very specific in your instructions, then get on with it. The longer you talk about role-playing as a technique and the more you talk about what might happen (or happened to you the last time you did it), the more you can raise anxiety in some group members who have never participated in such an event.

1. Assign specific roles to people[2]. Call for volunteers, or ask individuals if you think they might do a good job in a part. Short written descriptions of less than 50 words can be helpful,

but don't set out whole scripts or lengthy role profiles. Give players a moment to read the material or to state what they think their role is to be.

2. Instruct those not involved in the play to situate themselves so that they can be observers.

3. Give observers clear instructions on what to look for, what to write down. They will be asked to report their observations after the role-play. Prepare the learners to be active observers!

4. Get the play started. If prepared roles are used, let the play run for a little while and then stop as soon as the point has been made. Unless your participants get stuck, it's best to stay out of the way while you jot down your own observations.

5. Put an end to the play with something like, "You seem to have reached a point where we can break," or, "Please take another two minutes and then we'll stop." Do all this before things get boring or the discussion too heated. Somewhere between 10 and 15 minutes seems about right for the typical role-play.

6. There are several ways to intensify a role-play by breaking in and directing the process.
   •One is *role reversal* where you ask players to change roles with others and continue the play in the new spot. This can be particularly interesting in "us vs. them" situations: players can now experience how the world looks from the other's viewpoint or different people can display different approaches to a given situation.

   •Another way to intervene is by way of a brief *interview* of the key player(s). You might ask a player, "How is the interview going for you?" or, "Do you want to take a different approach? What would you like to do differently?" or, "Let me make a suggestion: look at the techniques we wrote on the flipchart earlier. Which one might help you get this interview flowing again?" Once the players have been given this little push, get out of the way and let the play take its natural flow.

   •A third intervention is based on *paradoxical intention*. Before asking players to "do it the right way," instruct them to go with what may come more easily. For instance, in a workshop on interviewing techniques you might say, "See if you can demonstrate an interviewer who really is *not* listening at all to the client." After a few minutes of the role-played interview, stop the action and invite the interviewer to switch and "now try to demonstrate as many active listening skills as you think might be appropriate."

3. De-briefing
1. Ask the role-players to report how things went for them. No long dissertations are needed here, just a quick summary from each, to hear their view of the situation while in role and at the same time to allow them the emotional release they might need to step out of the role.

2. Assist players to step out of their roles; sometimes asking them to change chairs and physically move away from their role is needed to have them rejoin the group.

3. Conduct a de-briefing. Ask observers to report what they saw and heard. Emphasize descriptions of actual behaviors over interpretations and second-guessing. If there is doubt, remind the group that "we have some expert witnesses here. Why don't we ask Fred what he felt when Marilyn confronted him about his doodling?" The clearer the instructions to the observers at the outset of the role-

play, the higher the quality of comments at this point.

4. Closure

Assist participants to integrate role-play results with material previously discussed. Have them answer the rhetorical question "So what?" or, "What can we say about effective ways of opening a meeting?"

This is also a good point at which to thank the role-players for taking the risk, and perhaps make some light-hearted comments about what happened. Avoid identification of individuals with certain roles: "Thank you, Margaret, for doing such a good job as an ineffective manager; I'm sure we all could see parts of ourselves in the way you portrayed that character."

Psycho-Social Drama

For those interested in accomplishing change, resolving conflicts and solving problems in organizational systems, a new strategy has been developed. Psycho-social Drama (PSD) is a mixture of drama and group process and has its roots equally in theatre, dramatic presentation, psychology, group dynamics and adult learning theory. PSD works like this. A team analyzes participant characteristics and expectations according to specific guidelines. These analyses are used to create one or more "units of action" or dramatic vignettes. Three levels of results are aimed for: sensitization, advocacy and problem-solving. The intensity of a unit is determined by the level of intent: lighter units for awareness/sensitization, heavily charged ones for problem-solving. Rather than studying methods and models of problem-solving, PSD creates an event that is powerful enough to start the problem-solving process on the spot. The units of action are carefully organized, rehearsed and presented. After five to eight minutes of presentation, the facilitator follows up with "directional processing" in which participants are guided through five stages: experiencing, sharing, interpreting, generalizing and applying.

This technique requires well-developed skills in group dynamics and process management and should be conducted by experienced trainers only.

For information, contact: Institute for Human Awareness, 1266 East Broad Street, Suite One West, Columbus, OH. Dee Mason and Jim Million are the developers of this technique.

Ten Tips For Constructing Role Plays

Use these if you want role-plays capable of developing specific skills in specific situations:

1. Determine the purpose of the simulated situation. List each ability you want participants to develop.

2. Design exercises which focus on the development of these abilities. The worth of a role-play depends on how successful you are in developing a script and role descriptions that suit specific objectives.

3. Outline the scenario. Decide on the name and nature of the simulated organization, number and type of roles. Sketch out the scenes of the roleplay.

4. Use a plot line and props that are believable and internally consistent. Use realistic characters, manuals and events, include rules and procedures which might be used in the actual setting.

5. Provide relevant roles for participants. The best role-plays replicate situations participants are familiar with. They ask roleplayers to assume parts for which they have the necessary technical and experiential background. Learners should see a job-related payoff in participating and acquiring skills.

6. Challenge participants. Ask them to generate alternatives as well as to choose among them. Train for the ability to propose options and criteria from which a decision will be made.

7. Check to see if the role-play fits the time available. Do participants have enough time to become familiar with the play, then analyse and generalize from it?

8. Give oral feedback. Emphasize positive features of each performance. Try serial role-plays—Act I, play, discussion; Act II, same roles, slightly altered situation, discussion.

9. Test the role-play with a small group, possibly one that has had experience in experiential techniques. Analyze strengths and weaknesses and make necessary changes.

10. Solicit feedback from participants. Ask how relevant the role-play was in developing X-skills, how realistic the scenario, the props, the role instructions?

From an article by H.L. Schachter in **Training and Development Journal.** February 1982. pp 9-10.

On page 61 I have described **structured** role-play, where you control at least the initial content of the scenario by scripting the setting and roles. In **unstructured** role-play the content of the play and the personalities of the characters emerge naturally from an event in the learning group[1].

Recommended To
- develop attitudes, opinions and feelings about certain persons and events.
- assist learners in developing insights into their own and others' motives and behaviors
- practice new behaviors involving stressful situations in a relatively safe setting.

Group Size and Physical Setting
Same as for Structured Role-Play.

Time Required
Between two and ten minutes.

Process
To use this style of role-play well, you have to have had some experience with the structured kind. The key here is spontaneity. In the midst of a discussion you suggest the use of a role-play, quickly set the scene, brief the players and get the thing rolling.

Although this is done with little formal preparation, the steps of de-briefing and closure need to be included, albeit in a shortened version.

Examples:

★ **To demonstrate a particular behavior.**

In a Basic Counseling Skills workshop, a participant has difficulty in explaining a type of client who occasionally presents a problem to her. The trainer suggests, "Why not give us a short demonstration of a situation involving such a client? Christine, think for a moment of a recent incident involving this kind of person. One of us will be the intake worker and you'll play the client." Two chairs are moved into the middle of the room, everybody shuffles chairs to get a good look, and off you go. As soon as a pattern emerges in the interview (or whenever Christine wants to), stop the action: "Is that the type of situation you were describing to us, Christine?" The role-play could end here if the trainer wanted to clarify the type of client only. If, however, this is also a good time to deal with ways of handling such clients better, the role-play could be continued: "Christine, would you try something? I'd like you to switch chairs now, be the intake worker. The other person ['OK with you, Fred?'] will now play the client in the manner you have demonstrated. Let's see how you handle the situation. Any time you feel you're getting stuck, or you wish you could try the interview over again, simply stop."

★ **To obtain insight into another's behavior**

During a Supervisory Skills workshop, two participants explain how they find it difficult to work together "when the pressure is on." The trainer suggests that it might be useful for both to experience the world from each other's viewpoint. A role-play is set up where the one takes the role of the other. They are instructed to have a conversation about their difficulty to function well under pressure. The trainer may take the third chair and act as a neutral third party to assist both role-players to talk about the problem while in the other's shoes.

After a few minutes of sharing their perceptions in this role reversal, the participants are asked to switch chairs and continue their conversation in light of the information they have just received.

★ **To try out unfamiliar behavior**

The trainer has just described several ways in which a job applicant might act more assertively during an interview: "I know it's easy for me to talk about these techniques. You are the ones that have to go out and be interviewed. You are probably skeptical of how they might work. Let's practice." She then sets the scene for a typical interview and asks one person to be the interviewer and another the applicant. The latter is instructed, "Just be yourself, the way you would in a normal interview. This time I'd like you to use the technique we have just discussed. Concentrate on that one technique alone and see how it suits you."

---

[1]Sources for prepared role-plays:
Maier, N. et al. **Supervisory and Executive Development: A Manual for Role-Playing.**
Annual Handbook for Facilitators. San Diego: University Associates. Annually since 1972.

[2] For a summary of each, see:
Wohlking W. and Weiner, H. "Structured and Spontaneous Role-Playing." **Training and Development Journal.** June 1981. pp 111-121.

Do you have a lot of material to cover and just don't have enough time to do it in? Do you want the participants to do preparatory work? Here are a few pointers.

Recommended To
- delegate to the learner responsibility for research of course material
- free the instructor to concentrate on essential or complex information
- emphasize that adults, given some guidance and encouragement, can manage their own learning
- develop an annotated reading list.

Caution
Adults are even less tolerant of "busy projects" than school children. The assignment has to be relevant and within the grasp of the learner. Most adults do not have experience in library research, nor do they have access to a library.

Group Size
Any.

Time Required
The reading or research is done outside regular class time, but there has to be time for the material to be presented and discussed in class.

Process
1. Define an area for additional reading or research. Students should be allowed to explore preferred areas if possible ("It's more exciting finding out things that I want, rather than those the instructor wants.")
2. Provide guidelines for what to look for, where to find it and what to do with the material.
3. Set firm completion dates and spell out consequences for late completion.
4. The reading/research material has to be put to use. This can be done by using buzz groups, team buzzes, representative presentations or a question-and-answer period.
5. Add additional information, clarify issues and correct false information.

Applications
- In a course where a great deal of current information can be gleaned from magazines and journals, certain students select one or two of the publications and regularly report to the class on relevant articles. The instructor, together with the class, then incorporates that information into the basic course material.
- A section of a text is assigned to be read prior to each class. Guiding questions help students to look for essentials and motivate them to look for peripheral issues. Class time is used to discuss, share questions and difficulties arising from material. Lecturettes provide additional material. At first I had fears that we would not have a high-quality course; I was giving much of the power for the success or failure of the course to the students. Naturally, the people who did not do their reading got less from the course than those who did. But that, as I had to remind myself and them, was their choice. During the discussions I was able to share much more of my expertise. The basics had already been covered through the readings. We also became a much closer group, all of us sharing some of the responsibility for the course's success.
Should you wish to try this, do it on a small scale first. You will probably have to be a "traffic cop" at first. Some people tend to take off on pet issues and arguments, while others may withdraw and feel that their time is wasted. You are still in charge of the course, but no longer the sole source of wisdom. What a relief, really! Just ask your students.

- A technique which I have used to get help in selecting a course text. A sample chapter from several texts under consideration is examined by students, who report to the whole class on the suitability of the text. They should especially be asked to look for: use of big words that could create problems, fluency of style, clarity of explanations, etc.
- Here are two sample handouts which you could adapt to your situation. The first "farms out" some of the course material to be dealt with by individual members, while at the same time building individualization into a course.

Mini-Paper

This "paper" can be done in writing or presented orally. It has two purposes: 1. For you to personalize this course by investigating a topic that holds particular interest for you; 2. for you to share your findings so that others in the group can learn from you.

How to select a topic?

As we move through the course and as you read the assignments, you may come across issues which are not being addressed in class to the degree you might like.

Possible issues:

(...list a few pertaining to your topic. The examples here are from a course on Discussion Leadership)

What is the significance of seating arrangements in meetings?

What leadership styles are most effective in task-oriented meetings?

What are the essential features of Robert's Rules of Order?

What are some problem-solving techniques that can be used in business meetings?

etc.

etc.

How to present your findings.

You have two options. You can either submit the issues and your findings to me in writing (for duplication and distribution to all participants), or you can book some time during the last two sessions to present your material so that we can get your first-hand account. My preference is for the second approach.

Whichever mode you select, make it lively, involving and useful. No dull stuff, please; you have probably had your share of sleep-inducing presentations in previous courses.

When is all this due?

_____

Late completions.

_____

Marks and Method of Evaluation:

_____

The second handout invites students to research the literature on a topic, select some items, prepare a brief critical description and submit it all in writing. Material will then be collated by the instructor (with the help of two or three participants) and distributed as an....

Annotated Bibliography

Your task is to peruse the literature on meeting management and such related areas as group dynamics, problem-solving, decision-making, conflict resolution, and small group leadership.

From the material you find of most value to yourself, and which you think would also interest the other participants, select

two books and two articles

and provide us with author/title information, a brief summary and critical comments. Total between 100 and 200 words per item. Assigned readings and handouts given during the course are to be excluded from your review list.

Your submission will be collected, collated into a reading list and distributed in time for the last week of the course.

Please use the following format for your submission:

Title: Author(s):	Name of journal or magazine: Book publisher: Date of publication or issue number:

A. Summary of Contents:

B. Your Critical Comments:

Locally available at:	Annotated by:

Due date:	Typewritten, single spaced.

Here is a way to utilize guest speakers, or experts within the ranks of the participant group.

Recommended To
- expose participants to the expertise of outside experts who discuss an issue in front of the class
- cast the learners in the role of "experts"
- put the spotlight on someone other than the instructor
- provide for structured interaction between panel and audience.

Class Size
Panel not more than any number in the audience.

Time Required
Long enough to make the desired points and to allow for discussion; if outsiders are invited, to make it worth their time and effort.

Materials Required
None.

Physical Setting
Arrange room and furniture as follows:

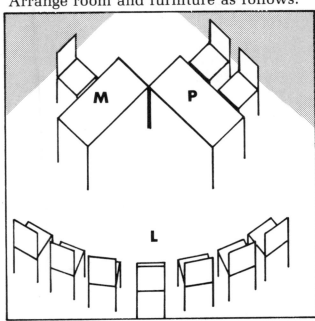

M—moderator (either instructor or student)
P—panel member
L—learners

Process
1. Select panel members and negotiate a topic or questions to which they are to speak.
2. Ensure that each panelist understands his role and is aware of the names, backgrounds and roles of other panelists. This can be done by telephone.
3. If course participants are to be the experts, go through the same procedure.
4. Meet with panel members (all together if that is possible) to review questions and procedures.
5. Help learners prepare for the event by brainstorming questions, advance readings, class discussions, or any method that would "prime the pump."
6. When the hour arrives:
   •arrange furniture (get help from your students)
   •introduce the panelists
   •act as moderator to keep things going and on task. Try not to dominate the discussion. Get the most from your panel.
7. During or after the panel presentation and discussion, initiate, direct, summarize interaction between the panel and group members.

Variation
Ask participants at the outset of a course to become experts on an aspect of the course. This will give individuals motivation to become involved, since they know their special turn will come. Instead of you being the sole fountain of information two or three students share that role.

Note: This technique is most useful if the learners take an active part in all aspects of the proceedings. Buzz groups, brainstorming or small discussion groups can be utilized in the planning, execution and follow-up of the panel debate.

The Self-Directed Adult Learner:
An Emerging Profile

Several studies have shown that:

★ about 80% of North American adults are involved annually in one or more organized "learning projects" (seven hours or more in length); 15% initiate their own learning.

★ adults are goal-oriented. Intentionality is a major characteristic of their learning.

★ adults prefer to pace and control the character of their learning experiences.

★ adults have varied learning patterns.

★ adults devote up to 900 hours to a single learning project, averaging 156 hours.

★ most adults prefer to study at home, although numerous other settings are used. Seventy percent of all learning projects are planned by the learner himself.

For more, see:

Tough, A. "Major Learning Efforts: Recent Research and Future Directions." **Adult Education,** Vol 28. pp. 250-263.

This is a variation on the panel debate.

Recommended To
- present different sides of a controversial issue, with equal time given to each side.
- let the audience interact with representatives from each side.

Group Size
Panel limited to either two speakers or the representatives of two groups; audience any size.

Time Required
Equal time for each side, plus time for audience interaction; from 10 minutes for an impromptu debate to one hour for prepared and more structured events.

Physical Setting
As in the following diagram:

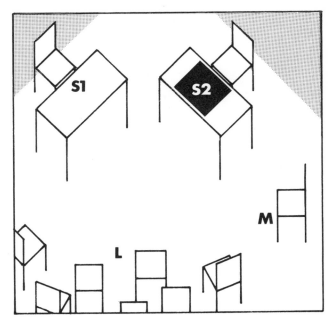

S1 & S2—opposing sides, opinions viewpoints (may be separated for effect)
M—moderator (you or a student)
L—learners

Caution
This can be an emotionally tense event. Allow time for flaring tempers to settle; people should go home stimulated, not exhausted or angry. Encourage and guide debating-team and audience interaction. If you ask a student to defend a given position ensure that the class recognizes this. As in **role-playing***, no one should end up being associated with an assumed role. This can be avoided by the following variation.*

Variation
After the first round of debate, ask the opposing sides to switch positions with each other and continue the discussion. This gives each person an appreciation of the other's position.

Recommended To
- provide first-hand observation of a process, procedure, event, etc., that could not be brought to the classroom in a better way
- make classroom instruction more meaningful through real-life reinforcement.

Group Size
Not more than 10 per guide. Larger classes should be broken up.

Time Required
Extra time required for planning the trip. If students travel on their own time, loss of class time is minimal.

Process
1. Make the arrangements well in advance and confirm them in writing. Visit the site yourself and discuss the planned event with those in charge.
2. If there is a guide, try to get to know the person and tell them about your group, their background and expectations. It is helpful if that person knows what you have been teaching and how this trip fits into the overall scheme.
3. Prepare your class by telling them about the site you plan to visit, why you are going there, and who will be there to meet them. The class as a whole can make a list of questions about the site.
4. Make sure everyone knows where to go on the date of the visits (emergency telephone contact, rides, material to bring, dress).
5. After the visit (or during your next class meeting), discuss the trip, give additional information and relate it to the course.
6. Send a note of thanks to your hosts; there is always next season's group to think of.

Keeping Journals During Field Projects

Placing students in work situations as part of their educational program requires regular communication between them and the instructor to make sure the experience is going well, and to see that the students are directed enough to be getting the most from the placement. Where regular face-to-face meetings may be difficult to arrange, the student journal may be the answer.

The coordinator of practicum placements at a New Canaan, CT school encourages students to be themselves and to express their feelings freely[1]. They are assured that no one but the coordinator will read the journal without their permission: "We are sometimes astonished at how honest the students can be in their journals."

For best results, a step-by-step framework is suggested; this encourages self-exploration and helps students develop specific observation and reporting skills. An outline could contain these headings:

1. Describe what you did in your placement today.
2. Describe your reaction to what you did today.
3. Describe the feedback you received from people you work with.
4. Describe your feelings and attitudes (about your observations).
5. Describe what you learned.
6. Describe what you would have changed about today's activity.
7. Describe things that are bothering you about the placement.

The journal entries may be used as starting points for discussion and progress evaluation: "Students frequently comment that, when they read the journals after some time has passed, they are surprised at how they felt and reacted. The writing not only helps them with recall, but also in clarifying feelings and attitudes."

[1]Zawacki, Vicki. "A Structure for Reflection." **Synergist.** Fall, 1981. p 47.

Field Project

Recommended To
- take the place of field trips when the class is too large or the time and location of the site is inconvenient
- provide in-depth observation and discovery.

Group Size
Individuals or groups of 2 to 3 people.

Time Required
Students arrange their own schedules.

Process
1. Discuss in class the purpose and outline of the project. This could be to: observe a manufacturing process, attend a function, observe/interview people, take photographs or tape recordings, collect materials/samples. Let learners choose their own projects as much as possible.
2. Provide assistance if required. *(letter of introduction, ideas, equipment, interview forms, rehearsal in class.)*
3. Agree on presentation/reporting format. This could be: a written report [standards?], oral report to whole class or sub-group, display of findings.
4. Agree on evaluation of the project. Does it count towards a course grade. How? Who 'marks'? (instructor, fellow students, the reporter or a combination).

Case in Point
In a training class for front office personnel in the hotel industry I switched from field trip to project. Rather than having 17 students follow a guide around a hotel (trying not be obvious; disturbing paying guests; attempting to hear the guide's explanations given in a hushed voice; missing half of the information because questions remained unanswered, etc.), students selected a hotel of the type in which they were likely to seek employment, made their own arrangements for a visit and experienced time actually working at the front desk. They had a letter of introduction from me and after that they were on their own. The results were satisfactory. Some were offered jobs on the spot, while others decided that perhaps this was not their kind of work. The course material was mostly verified, sometimes questioned, but in all cases made more meaningful.

Journals: Diaries for Growth

How can you arrange it so that your students get full use of their learning activities, both in class and outside it? In the continuing search for ways to enrich adult learning, journals—sometimes called logs, diaries or plain notebooks—may be a simple yet effective tool.

Synergist magazine[1] published a collection of articles in which instructors familiar with the use of diaries reported their experiences. Their course topics ranged from theology to psychology, from sociology to English, from supervisory skills to hospital volunteering. Here is a summary of their comments.

At Boston College[2] undergraduates are assigned one of 35 different placements, from tutoring Laotian refugees to working in a residential setting with abused children. For many students, this represents the first serious challenge to their previously established opinions, values and priorities. Their course provides a structure through which students are asked to examine the failures of institutions and the effect these have on the life of individuals. By using journals, students find an outlet for their troubling questions and their own feelings. The instructor needs to be sensitive to the confidential nature of journal entries and must respond in an appropriate manner. Once the professor has established trust with the student, she can begin to pose alternative ways of looking at problems.

In the community involvement program at Macalester College, St. Paul[3], students are encouraged to organize journals thematically in a looseleaf binder. Some themes may reflect the writer's personal life (such as dreams, fears and relationships), others may reflect aspects of relationships with institutions, job or education. Within each theme, the students may include detailed subcategories, pertaining to either work/practicum or academic life. They may include goals, tasks, strategies and self-evaluation of development. "Be ritualistic," students are told. "Set aside a time every day for reflection and writing. Be analytical. Allot 20% of writing time for stating the problem and 80% for solving it. Be optimistic. Just because a placement falls apart does not mean you cannot learn something valuable from it."

Journals can also be used to stimulate small group discussion. With the writer's consent, the instructor asks the students to examine an instance or problem from her journal. Verbalizing, sharing and exchanging ideas enhances learning from experience and adds to the development of trust in the learner group.

As students become more experienced at journal writing, the instructor can urge them to avoid mere reporting of feelings and impressions and concentrate instead on their objective observations and judgement, and the integration of experience with theory.

Synergist. Fall 1981. 46-49. Five articles are presented in that issue, two are excerpted here.

[2]Jane Zimmerman ("Journal as Dialogue") is an administrative intern at Boston College, Chestnut Hill, MA.

[3]Charles Norman ("Journal as Discipline") is director of the Learning Skills Center at Macalester College, St. Paul.

Additional Reading

These publications are recommended in the **Synergist** article.

Progoff, Ira. **At a Journal Workshop.** 1975 Dialogue House, 80 East 11th Street, New York 10003. 320 pages, $7.95.
Describes Progoff's intensive journal technique. In a followup book, **The Practice of Process Meditation** (1980, 343 pages, $7.95) he gives a method for psychological self-care that has a spiritual base.

Rainer, Tristine. **The New Diary.** 1979. J.P. Tarcher, 9110 Sunset Blvd. Los Angeles, CA 90006. 320 pages, $5.95.
Presents a system for keeping journals, progressing from fairly simple to advanced techniques. Includes discussions of relationship of journal-keeping to creative processes.

Baldwin, Christine. **One-to-One.** 1979. M.Evans & Co. Inc., 216 East 49th Street, New York, NY 10017. 186 pages, $3.95.
Introduces the journal process, starting with basics and proceeding to an in-depth discussion of key areas in which journals can be effective.

Recommended To
- help learners keep track of their experiences during a course or workshop and learn from them
- collect material for an evaluation session at various stages of the course
- assist learners in relating course material and events to their personal lives and work.

Group Size
Any. This is an individual exercise. The sharing of the information is optional and can be done using one of the small group strategies described in the KIT.

Time Required
Any number of five to 10 minute periods during class time, and the participants' own time.

Materials
Ask learners to keep a section of their notebook/binder or a separate little booklet for these notes.

Process
1. Introduce the idea of a diary or journal as a way of recording personal impressions, experiences, discoveries and questions as the course progresses.
2. Point out the private nature of these entries, but say that you would appreciate it if people would share their entries with the class, certain individuals or yourself; either at certain times during the course or at the end.
3. Give an example of what might go into the journal and how to record events. Samples on the next pages.
4. Answer questions but keep it short and low key; ask participants to suspend judgement on this new experience and see how it might work out.

5. At specified points in the course allow time so that participants can make entries in their journals. With groups that have had little or no experience in this reflective approach to learning, provide key questions to guide them through the exercise.
6. *[Optional]* Invite individuals to share whatever they wish with either a "buddy" or groups of 3 to 5 others. This "publishing" of journal material can serve as a subtle evaluation of both content and process of the course.

Note
Journals don't have to be kept for the entire course. Examples #2 and #3, for instance, are suitable for recording reflections on specific events in the program. All three examples stress:
- reflection
- analysis
- plan for action.

Example #1
*(with **headings** provided by the instructor)*

Date: _____   Topic: _____

What Happened:

Today Peter mentioned that we were required to visit a hotel and arrange for a four-hour practicum. We are supposed to do it at a place where we would like to work some day. He said he wouldn't make the arrangements for us, but gave us a letter of introduction. The rest is up to each of us.

How I feel/felt about it:

I am not sure if I like this: going to a strange place to ask such a favour makes me nervous. What if they are too busy? What sort of place would I like to visit? Maybe this would be a good exercise for me to see if I really like the hotel business. Peter says that the people are usually very friendly.

Action Plan:

I will look at the list of hotels Peter gave us and pick two that appeal to me. I'll go to each sometime before the next class, just to have a look around. From these impressions, I'll pick the place I like best. Then I might be ready to make that phone call.

Example #2
Self-evaluation and Completion of the Learning Loop[1]

Date: _____   *Topic:* _____

A. *What questions do you have as a result of your learning experience today? Jot these down below.*

B. *From these questions, what* **key concepts** *can you extrapolate for further learning? Write these concepts below.*

C. *How can you go about finding answers to the questions you raised above? Jot down at least one specific approach you will take:*

_____

Example #3
Self-evaluation and reflection
(from a Discussion Techniques workshop)

Date: _____   *Role:* _____

A. *Looking back over this morning's session, what did you learn about the way groups work together?*

B. *What did you (re-)discover about your own behavior in groups?*

C. *What changes, if any, do you wish to make in your behavior while working in small task groups?*

D. *How will you know that you have been successful in making the desired change(s)?*

[1]*From David Kolb, et al.* **Organizational Psychology**. *2nd edition. Englewood Cliffs: Prentice-Hall. 1974.*

Tips for Using Films

The following techniques could be useful to help your learners integrate the film's message with the rest of the course material. They are designed for small group tasks (three to six people) and require between five and 30 minutes of class time.

To frame questions. A relatively elementary use of the group is to "buzz" or discuss the film with the objective of coming up with a question which the film seems to raise. The question may be answered by another group, the group at large, or possibly yourself.

To specify learning. Another easy way to put the group to work is to ask them to zero in on one or two important ideas which are introduced in the film. In effect, the group is challenged to think in terms of "what have we learned?"

To respond to specific questions. You may wish to have the small groups focus on specific questions raised by the film. The questions may be distributed to participants via a question sheet prepared in advance of the film session, or they may be written on the chalkboard or large newsprint. You may give each small group one or two questions of a special sort, or all small groups may work on the same question(s). Depending on the available time, the process may be repeated a second time or more.

Brainstorming. The film may introduce a problem which can be worked on in a brainstorming way. A group of 6 to 12 people, plus a recorder to capture the ideas, works out well. You might serve as a recorder or the recorder might be drawn from the group, depending on the number of groups at work.

To critique assigned readings. Provide a pertinent article or handout and ask for it to be discussed in relation to the film.

To relate to back-home problems. Encourage reflections on back-home problems, areas requiring change, etc. Assign small groups the task of identifying two or three of their most significant problems, or ask for an unlimited, open-ended list of problems.

To function as general viewing teams. Assign small groups specific viewer roles and require them to comment on the film with these openers: the *questioners*: "The film raises these questions for us." The *clarifiers*: "The film contradicted the text's contention that..." Or, "There was some confusion regarding..." The *disagreers*: "We were turned off by..." Or, "We don't agree with..." The *agreers*: "We respond positively to..." Or, "We agree with..." The *appliers*, "We can see these applications..."

To assess personal effectiveness. Participants can be invited to assess their own behavior in situations similar to those in the film. For instance, a group of supervisors viewing a film on management skills could work on a task to determine their difficulties with delegation. Or, in a communication skills development film, "The times when I made some of the errors depicted in the film." (This approach involves self-disclosure on the part of participants and should not be used until a sufficient level of trust has been developed.)

This involves more than threading the film and turning off the lights. For films to be real partners in the facilitation of learning, they need to be carefully selected, presented and followed up.

Recommended To
- provide alternative information channels for student (low reading skills required)
- provide a continuity of action; showing it exactly as it occurs, sometimes reducing long demonstration processes to brief sequences
- provide a "front seat" for many events, processes and experiences. Experts can perform demonstrations, equipment can be made available, places can be visited, and everything in color, at the right angle and speed for analysis and learning. Films can be stopped at certain points for summary, discussion, questioning. They can be reshown or viewed by individual learners in the library.

Caution
★ *Films quickly become outdated and lose their impact on the viewers. Also, their established rate and method of presenting the material forces all learners to follow it at the same speed and with the same level of comprehension; some may become bored while others may find the material too difficult or abstract.*

★ *The image shows best on the screen when the lights are turned off, but this precludes note-taking (and might encourage naps). Effective use of films requires careful planning by the instructor. Use them not just for their entertainment value, but be clear on how they contribute to learning.*

Process
1. Plan:
   •Find out what films are available (library, trade and professional associations, consultants, film board).
   •Are the available films (according to their description) appropriate for your objectives?
   •If so, is the film up-to-date, realistic? Do you agree with its content, or does it present a desired alternative approach to the subject?
2. Make the arrangements:
   •Book the film in advance and preview it.
   •Book a projector and screen and check if room can be darkened. Make sure you know how to work the projector.
   •Check the classroom seating arrangement to make sure it is suitable for film viewing.
3. Prepare learners:
   •Relate the film to the course content. Explain its setting, peculiarities if any, and quiz students on relevant background information.
   •Inform students of what they can expect to see and learn from this film.
   •Instruct viewers to look for specific problem areas illustrated in the film, e.g., for a management training film one small group might be asked to look specifically at non-verbal communication, another group may be asked to observe areas which relate to team building.
   •Inform students how the film's content will be used in the course: is it to present new information, to illustrate previously-made points, to entertain, or . . .?
4. Show the Film:
   •Avoid fumbling with the focus, sound and other mechanical details. Rehearse if necessary.
   •You may want to stop at certain points ("Sorry to wake you up!"), to raise a point, elicit questions or receive reactions regarding its content and presentation.
   •Try to leave some of the room lights switched on to permit note-taking.

5. Follow-up:
   •Begin by inviting questions and comments. Do not get too wrapped up in discussions of its cinematographic qualities, go straight to the issues for which you chose the film.
6. Keep a record:
   •Course name, audience profile, at what point of the proceedings you showed the film and how you introduced it, what activities followed, plus other comments to help you make good use of the film the next time around (or avoid ever using it again).

One of the most easily available visual aids, aside from the chalkboard, is the overhead projector. Transparencies for use on the overhead projector can easily be prepared either by drawing directly onto the transparent acetate or by using one of the many office duplicating machines that offer this capability. Unusual effects such as silhouettes and cut-outs are also easily prepared. Two superimposition methods are possible: one involves stacking transparences layer upon layer thus illustrating complex models and processes as you talk about them. The other method involves projecting an image onto a writing surface (chalkboard) and adding in the details by writing on that surface.

Advantages

- You can operate the unit from the front of the room while facing the audience.
- The transparency placed face up on the top of the machine is completely legible to you and serves as notes (including "reminders" written on the transparency's cardboard frame).
- When equipped with a roll of transparency sheeting, the unit can serve as a projected chalkboard. Material written on the sheeting can be stored for re-use as is, or cleaned off and used again.
- Presentation is easily modified by the deletion or insertion of transparencies.
- The time spent on each item is completely under your control. The lamp can be switched on or off to project the image at certain times of your presentation. A transparency can be "brought back" at the end of the presentation or at a later class session for review and/or to stimulate recall and discussion.
- Room lights remain on giving learners no time to snooze, and easy opportunity to take notes.

Disadvantages

- Overhead projectors are awkward bits of machinery and they may create a barrier between you and your class.
- Instructors have been known to fall in love with this device and use it at the slightest provocation. Talking directly to the class, writing a word or two on the chalkboard or flip-chart, giving handouts and other proven techniques are not to be discounted in favour of this, or other, "gadgets."

Making Transparencies

You can either write directly on transparency sheets or use an office duplicating machine capable of copying onto transparencies. With the first method use special marking pens (they are available in many colors) which can be water-based (erasable) or alcohol-based (permanent). With the second method a clean original has to be made first, then copied in either black & white or full color. The latter is the most expensive way to go. (Check with your company or school audio-visual department. Quick-printers also offer this service).

In any case, the design of the visual should follow these basic guidelines:

Size: The usable surface of a standard transparency frame is 7½" x 9½", so your prepared copy cannot exceed these dimensions. If you wish to use it without the cardboard frame, you can plan on having an 8" x 10" working area.

Simplicity: Keep your design simple. Complete details can be confusing and unnecessary since you will be there to explain.

- Use no more than six words per line and six or fewer lines per image.
- Select key words and phrases. Don't try to recap the entire presentation on one transparency.
- Space lines by at least 1 ½ to 2 lines.
- Use simple, bold lettering types, at

least ¼" high. Sans serif types are best. Typewritten material does not project well.

- If the original can be read at a distance of 10 feet, the transparency should project well.
- Horizontal is considered the best format, although vertical is acceptable. Here is a suggestion for good transparency layout:

Pacing: Don't show more information than is necessary at one time. If you show too much, your audience will be ahead of you and lose attention in the specific point you are making.

- Use the transparencies as your lesson notes. If you use cardboard frames, additional key words can be written there, only for you to see.
- Use the revelation technique by placing a sheet of heavy paper under the transparency. By moving the sheet down you reveal the image line-by-line and thus can control the viewers' attention.
- Use a pen or pointer on the transparency to direct attention to specific points. Avoid pointing at the screen (thus turning your back to the audience and having to look close up

at the very bright screen), place your pen or a flat, pointed object directly on the projection surface. The shadow will show on the screen and leave your hands free. Avoid "dancing" all of the image with the pointer or your hands, as this can irritate the viewers.

- Use overlays to provide a sense of progression. Up to four transparencies can be placed upon each other in succession.
- Turn the projector on and off while changing transparencies or whenever you want to redirect the attention of the group away from the image and back to you. Light tends to attract more than you do, so beware of the competition.

Room set-up

Rarely will you have the ideal physical setting, but make a point of checking the room beforehand and arranging the furniture to suit your needs.

This is the standard classroom. All too often the screen is mounted so that it sits in the middle of the front wall, right behind the instructor's desk and just so that it obscures the chalkboard when pulled down. Who designed that arrangement, the purchasing department?

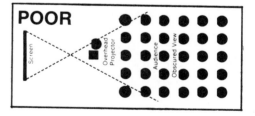

Don't be stuck with this set-up! See if you can get a portable screen and put it off to the side. Suggested arrangements:

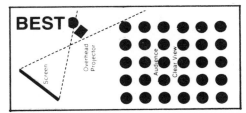

When using an overhead projector, arrange the room so the audience's view of the screen is not obstructed

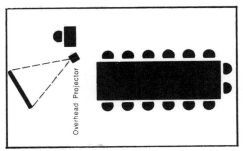

Centre table arrangement. Suitable for under 20 people. This set-up promotes discussion and is best for long meetings.

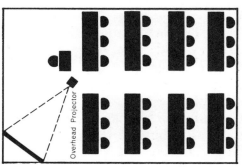

Classroom arrangement. This is a standard arrangement suitable for any size group.

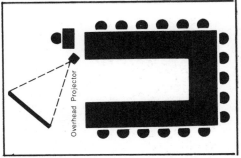

U-table arrangement. Suitable for 30 people or fewer. This arrangement is ideal for group discussion and interaction.

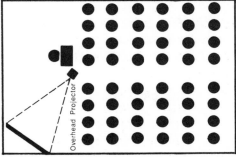

Auditorium/theater arrangement. (Single projector). Suitable for any size audience, but most efficient for large groups.

Auditorium/theatre arrangement. (Dual projectors). As above, this arrangement works well with large groups. Two projectors and screens give the presenter more latitude in his presentation.

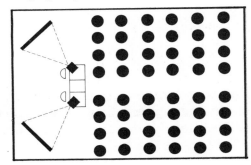

"The truly creative individual stands ready to abandon old classifications and to acknowledge that life, particularly his own unique life, is rich with new possibilities."

—*Frank Barron*

Reg Herman,
Department of Adult Education.
Ontario Institute for Studies in Education

Planning for Learning:
A Model for Creative Decision Making

Every planning experience and every job, including teaching, can be dealt with in three ways: one, shrink it; two, do it efficiently and well; or three, expand it. As adult educators, we enjoy real freedom to be creative decision-makers in our planning: to clarify values on social issues, to expand our goals and experiment with methods of evaluation, to invent learning methods that meet the learners' needs and go beyond to encourage the learners to become 'masters of their own destiny'[1]. This is what I mean by a model for creative decision-making, but I think the best way to understand and assess my approach is to compare with other models of planning in adult education: the classic model, Malcolm Knowles' and Ginny Griffin's. On the way, there are three key issues that the decision-making model raises.

This may surprise you, but the most frustrating issue for me is: where do you start? and with that comes the question of social responsibility. The second issue is when and how to get evaluation into the act without breaking your back in requirements of time and energy. The third is two-fold: what is creativity, and how do you apply creative problem-solving and decision-making to planning in adult education.

THE CLASSIC PLANNING MODEL

In education, planners promote a myth that there is a five-step sequence that goes like this:

     Conduct needs assessment
     Set learning objectives
     Choose methods and resources
     Implement
     Evaluate

Sometimes this model is drawn as a horizontal continuum, sometimes a circle, but in effect the sequence always *ends* with evaluation and my theory is that's why no one ever does it. By the time they get to the end, they're too tired!

Planning for learning is not a linear sequence. Typically, it's a back-and-forth flow of problem-solving and decision-making. It's not unusual for planners to choose their techniques before deciding what it is they're going to do. Frequently, the length of the course is decided first (five days, 36 hours, three evenings), and then decisions are made to fill the time. Perhaps it doesn't matter where you begin in the classic model, but I suggest you don't start by filling time. The first course I ever planned began just there, we filled a week. Coming from a business background, however, I was brash enough to evaluate every session and the total course with pre- and post-tests. The results were a disaster. Participants learned nothing and intended to change nothing. But I learned two things: One, never start by filling time; and two, evaluate everything. I would never have known the mistakes if I had not been determined to evaluate every session.And another thing: keep your results; in the long run they will be your best measure of how you're developing as a planner and facilitator.

MALCOLM KNOWLES' MODEL

To the classic model, Knowles contributed two important additions, and in so doing, he changed the focus from 'pedagogy' to 'andragogy.' He defines andragogy as the art and science of helping adults (or better, maturing human beings) learn. He equates pedagogy with teacher-directed learning and contrasts it with andragogy, self-directed learning[2].

Knowles comes to the planning function with a value system that esteems the knowledge and skills that adults acquire through life experience. He defines the adult educator as a colleague of and co-learner with his/her students, a facilitator who works with the learners to help them identify their learning needs, set their own objectives, choose methods appropriate to their learning styles and the way that they wish to evaluate their progress.

One of his goals as a planner follows directly: he must plan how to *involve* the learners in the planning! This was Knowles' first addition to the classic model, and it led to the need for the second. For most adults, to be involved in planning their own learning in a classroom situation is a radical change; they have been conditioned to accept the teacher as an authority who tells the students what to think and what to do. As a good problem-solver, Knowles took a step back and recognized that the *first* thing to plan is a learning environment that will help the participants change, a learning climate that will be informal, supportive, conducive to developing mutual respect and trust. This is the way his model looks:

> Set climate
> Devise mutual planning
> Diagnose needs
> Set objectives
> Plan methods and resources
> Implement
> Evaluate for re-planning

GINNY GRIFFIN'S MODEL

In the best adult education style and consistent with her own prescriptions, Griffin's[3] approach is continuously evolving and therefore difficult to render in abridged form. Nevertheless, she clearly adds three more ideas. First of all, she draws attention to the great fact of decision problems: all down the line of the planning process there are choice points and it is the responsibility of the adult educator *qua* planner to be aware of the consequences of each choice.

Second, she brings the planner's and institution's educational philosophies up front where they belong in problem-solving and decision-making, and after the process she raps the planner on the head and charges him/her: be aware of what you believe about education and learning, and behave in your work-life planning in ways consistent with those beliefs. Finally, she challenges the planner to continue to learn and change.

REG HERMAN'S MODEL

This model proposes three additional strategies for planning in adult education.

First, here we are again with where do you start? I think it's clear that all of us operate from a value base; the trouble is that we don't make our values explicit, so they don't help us in our decision making. Furthermore, Paulo Freire has shown us that there is no neutral education[4] and that adult educator-planners must deal with this responsibility. So, in this model we *front-end* all problem-solving and decision-making with the clearest possible public statement of our personal, educational and social values, and link them to our planning goals.

Second, this model seeks to turn planning outside in, to bring the planning of evaluation in from the cold and join it to the goals and objectives. This way, we increase the chances that the planner will actually conduct evaluations and, as you will see, we will also improve the clarity of the goals and therefore the likelihood of congruence between values and goals and methods.

Third, it is not enough for the planner merely to be aware of alternatives. In this model, the planner actively searches for all the information about known alternatives and then goes beyond even that, to *invent* further alternatives still, especially alternative goals, but also alternative methods.

•"Neutral Adult Education"

All educational planning, including the planning of leisure courses, is a political act. To put it simply, education that does not seek to change conditions reinforces the existing system.

•Creative Burnout

Even if we grant the adult educator-planner that the planning of a course in astronomy, say, is non-political, the lack of values is still self-defeating: planning that is not front-ended by a defined value system is trivialized. William Gordon, inventor of the creative problem-solving strategy called Synectics, found that, after a time, his best problem-solving teams dried up. He thought their creativity had burned out. I think he's wrong and that his teams simply were not willing or able to go on spending enormous creative energies to invent new bottle tops and other gadgets for industry.

I suspect that the current phenomenon of teacher burnout would reveal a similar gap. People are turned on by creative challenges, but they need to feel that their efforts are contributing to significant values. Faced with problem-solving and decision-making that are not front-ended by her or his values, the planner will either fail to spend the time necessary for good planning or will burn out.

•A Value Base for Self-Directed Learning

There is no one right way of teaching, but there are many strong arguments for planning self-directed elements into adult education and training programs[356]. There is also a value base to this planning decision.

One of the reasons that so many people don't hark back to Proposition One of decision-making: **they don't believe or perceive that they have an alternative.** These people disenfranchise themselves from life's options. It follows that a first concern—the mission and purpose—of adult education is to help people gain greater decision-making power over their lives and destinies, and this includes or leads to increased commitment to and control over their communities and society. (Just think for a moment about the reasons why your students come to your course, and how they hope to gain opportunities for growth by acquiring new skills and knowledge. This applies equally to career, academic or leisure courses.)

As adult educators we construct the educational step towards these goals by planning programs that help participants gain control over their own learning, by designing structures and processes that give them increasing responsibility for their learning *within* the educational program you design. The following scale oversimplifies our alternatives but it's useful in comparing teaching approaches. I'd like to invite you to do two things: first, add to this continuum other teaching methods or program designs, for example, Socratic teaching, experiential learning, and so on. Second, place your own planning and/or teaching style on the scale.

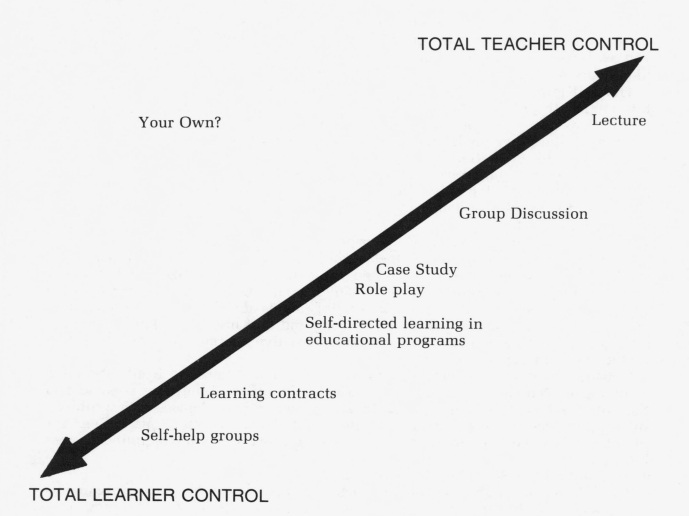

TOTAL TEACHER CONTROL

Your Own?

Lecture

Group Discussion

Case Study
Role play

Self-directed learning in
educational programs

Learning contracts

Self-help groups

TOTAL LEARNER CONTROL

A recent survey of adult students showed that those who developed learning contracts experienced the greatest sense of control over their learning. I'd be very interested in your additions to the scale and your comments about what I have said in this introduction to planning.

•The Distinction between Goals and Objectives

Most planners find it useful to distinguish the term goals, the broader statement of purpose, from objectives, the more precise aims to achieve those goals. When you develop an educational event (course, workshop, seminar) on the topic "Managing Meetings Better," you might have the goal: to improve the quality of meetings held in the organization. You might also have the goal: to develop such a course so that it would protect and support the self-confidence of the participants by designing self-paced learning whenever feasible.

The objectives could fall in one of three categories: planning objectives, learning objectives and process objectives. Examples are:

planning objectives: that the course be ready by a certain date;
that the course be not longer than two days;
that the new video equipment be used.

learning objectives:	that the learner be able to:
	define the difference between process and content;
	describe ten common meeting problems and how to solve them;
	build an agenda.
process objectives[7]	that the learners:
	develop confidence in running a meeting;
	enjoy working together and sharing information with each other;
	assume greater resposibility for their own learning.

• Bring Evaluation In From the Cold

In the early seventies, the Maryland Department of Education produced 24 videotapes for the training of adult education teachers. When they were ready to implement the program they called in external evaluators. I'm sure you can guess the complaint in the evaluators' report: if they had been called in when the planning began, they could have helped the planners and conducted a more detailed and useful evaluation. On the other hand, they should have been grateful: precious few adult education programs conduct *any* evaluation.

One of the reasons why adult educators don't evaluate is because they don't want to hear the bad news—even though they know it's the only way they can hope to learn what to change and improve their planning and teaching. Evaluation can also cost too much, in terms of money, time and energy. (Just reflect: when do you normally evaluate your courses? Who does it? How much influence do the participants have? What do you do with that information—during the course and afterwards?).

So here are two tricks I'd like to recommend: (1) write your statements of goals and objectives in behavioral terms and so specifically and precisely that evaluation is literally built in to them—you'll make it or you won't, and you'll *know*; (2) keep your evaluation short and simple and use many different strategies.

More on how to write objectives on page 98.

More on how to do in-course evaluations on pages 121 to 127.

To sum up on evaluation: decision-making always involves risk; the planner clarifies her or his values and goals, identifies and generates alternatives and revises the goals, conducts vigilant information searches and so seeks to make the best possible decision. In the absence of that guarantee, the planner *must evaluate or go on making the same mistakes ad infinitum.*

• Applying Creativity in the Model

There are really two levels of creativity in the planning process. One is to make new connections, the other is to expand the frontiers, to invent new options. If, as a planner, you conduct a search to identify alternative learning goals and methods, you may use imagination in seeking out information about goals and methods from colleagues, from similar programs in others' organizations, from the journals—in other words, using your resources well. The author of **Decision Making** calls that "vigilant information search"[8]. But that is not being creative. It becomes a creative act when you synthesize ideas you have generated from different sources into new connections for your own planning.

But when you push still further to generate and invent alternative goals and objectives, this brings together both originality and imagination in planning a creative leap. Brainstorming (page 47) is one enjoyable method of using small groups to generate a great quantity of ideas.

One caveat: unlike education, creativity is neutral. In fact, very nasty people have found monstrous ways of being creative. So there is nothing casual about the insistence that creative decision-making be inextricably linked to a clear value system.

REG HERMAN'S PLANNING MODEL FOR CREATIVE DECISION-MAKING

1. *Identify the values* implicit in the decisions to conduct the program. Put them in writing.
2. Survey the full range of possible *goals.* Deliberately generate alternatives, for example, by Brainstorming.
3. Use all your resources to conduct a vigilant information search for the *objectives* of the program. These objectives serve as a reference base for your values and goals.
4. Decide on your program's *goals* and *objectives* and relate them to some criteria. Check: are they so clear that *evaluation* is built in, so clear that the participants will be able to say, "we made it"—or—"we didn't"? Start planning your *evaluation* strategies.
5. Thoroughly canvass the spectrum of alternative *learning methods* (called Instructional Techniques in this KIT). Brainstorm new ones. Use creative problem-solving, make new connections.
6. *Name Your Decisions—to Change, to Invent, to Adventure....*

In conclusion, a personal note. This article began as a reminder that there is no neutral education. That's true, but it doesn't mean that planning can't be fun! I hope this model assists you, as it has me, to enjoy continuous challenges in your work. Finally, this model invites you to risk naming all your decisions. That's not only good planning, it's a great satisfaction.

This article was adapted for use in the KIT. It is the substance of a chapter in a book to be published by the Ontario Centre for Studies in Education.

NOTES & REFERENCES

[1] This is the title of the book by Moses M. Coady, describing the Antigonish Movement, one of the most effective adult education movements in Canada.

[2] Knowles, Malcolm, S. **The Modern Practice of Adult Education.** 2nd edition. New York: Association Press. 1980.

[3] Griffin, Virginia, R. "Self-Directed Adult Learners and Learning," in **The Design of Self-Directed Learning.** Reg Herman (ed.), 2nd edition. Toronto: O.I.S.E., 1982.

[4] Freiro, Paulo. **Education for Critical Consciousness.** New York: Seaburg, 1973.

[5] Knowles, Malcolm. **Self-directed Learning.** New York: Association Press, 1975.

[6] Tough, Allen. "Post Secondary Applications," **The Design of Self-Directed Learning,** Reg Herman (ed.), Toronto: O.I.S.E., 1982.

[7] For more on the separation of learning and process objectives, see: Eisner, Elliot. **The Educational Imagination.** New York: Macmillan, 1979, chapter 6.

[8] Janis, Irving and Leon Mann, **Decision Making.** New York: Free Press, 1977.

[9] Koberg, Don and Jim Bagnall. **The Universal Traveler.** Los Altos, CA: William Kaufmann Inc., 1976. page 6.

[10] Adams, James L. **Conceptual Blockbusting.** (2nd edition), Toronto: George J. McLeod, 1979.

[11] de Bono, Edward. **PO: Beyond Yes and No.** New York: Penguin, 1972. **A Five Day Course in Thinking.** New York: Penguin 1969.

A delightfully crazy book, **The Universal Traveler**[9] gives a wide range of problem-solving techniques and proposes the following sequence in the design process (p. 17):

Accept the situation—
To accept the problem as a challenge; to give up our autonomy to the problem and allow the problem to become our process.

Analyze—
To get all the facts and feelings; to get to know what the world of the problem looks like.

Define—
To decide what we believe the main issues to be; to conceptualize and to clarify our major goals concerning the problem situation.

Ideate [sic]**—**
To generate options for achieving the essential goals; to search out all the ways of possibly getting to the major goals. Alternatives.

Select—
To choose from the options; to relate our goals to our possible ways of getting there. Determine best ways to go.

Implement—
To give action or physical form to our selected "best ways."

Evaluate—
To review and plan *again*; to determine the effects or ramifications as well as the degree of progress of our design activity.

Another place to find ideas is in **Conceptual Blockbusting**[10] and the books by Edward deBono[11].

Creative thinkers make many false starts, and continually waver between un-manageable fantasies and systematic attack.

—Harry Hepner

A Trusty 10-Step Planning Model

Reg Herman warns us, on page 89, to beware of simplistic planning models. Nonetheless, I give you my handy model and invite you to make it yours. Use it to plan any educational event, be it a one-day workshop, a ten-session evening course, or a two-semester college course.

However...
- add or delete parts to suit you.
- don't go too far in planning (and don't start to instruct) unless you first have a clear picture of your objectives. What are you aiming for?
- no one method is best for all groups. Beware of your pet methods and weak spots and try to avoid them.
- aim to be less a sole provider of knowledge and more a helper in the adults' learning efforts. This way you will be able to attend to their varying needs, demands and talents.
- remember, it is your plan and you can change it. Try to learn from the decisions you make as the changes occur.
- don't use the model in a linear fashion: start anywhere, go clockwise and anti-clockwise; just try to cover all points at some time.

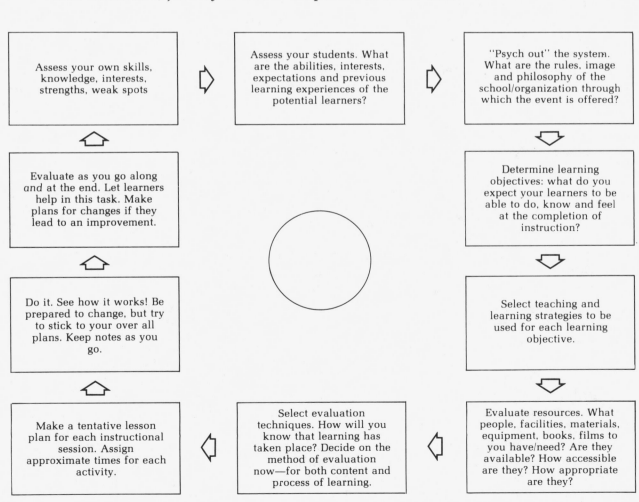

Let's have a closer look at the 10 steps:

Step #1: Your Own Skills. . .

You are the center of the plan and the course. Your personality, your attitude, your communication skills, your knowledge and experience as the "expert" and teacher are all essential contributions to the plan. By taking an inventory of what you are bringing to the course, you can pin-point strengths and weaknesses. Ask: How can I use my strengths? How can I best share my experience with the learners? How can I share the load? Which areas give me trouble in this course? Who (what) can help? What happened during the last course? What went well and what needs work?

Step #2 The Learners' Skills. . .

Ask: How can I get a clearer picture of my prospective students? Can colleagues help? When I taught the course before, who attended? What type of person is likely to respond to the calendar course announcement? What will she expect, bring with her, hope to gain, be prepared to share?

Step #3 The System. . .

The agency, company or school which sponsors the course often influences who comes, what is expected, and what is likely to happen in the classroom. Is this a relaxed, formal, old-fashioned, liberal, academic, or happy type of place? What are the rules that will affect your course? What are the administrative constraints? With points 1, 2 and 3 sketched out, you now have a fairly good idea of the people that will be involved and also know of some of the dynamics that will govern your course.

Step #4 Your Instructional Objectives. . .

The most useful (if tedious) way to start planning the actual course content is to consider the final product. Use the analogy of baking a cake: by looking in the recipe book, you might start off with the name of the product and a color illustration. Next to it will be a list of ingredients, some preparatory steps, and a detailed outline of how to mix the ingredients, work the equipment, etc. Eventually, there is talk of decorations, serving and *voila!* the enjoyment of the finished cake. I don't think the planning of courses should differ much. The following simple rules for defining the objectives will help you plan towards the final "product."

•*Decide what you expect the students to be able to do, know, think and feel by the end of the course (or a section of it).*

Avoid vague statements such as "The student will appreciate the steps of baking a cake." Or, "My aim is to teach the basic skills of cake baking." Instead, ask yourself, "What are the basic skills of cake baking? What can a person do with these skills? Could one expect to be able to bake a cake, follow certain rules, apply certain methods, manipulate certain tools and supplies? What are they and with what degree of expertise could one expect to manage all these skills? What background knowledge would such a "baker" need to handle unusual events, or variations to the recipe? What attitudes (regarding sanitation and safety) would someone have to display when preparing the cake? What feelings (about color or taste, of enjoyment or pride) would be desirable side effects of cake baking?"

Enough of cakes. This peculiar way to look at objectives can be applied successfully to any type of learning, however complex. If you start from the final product and work backwards, it will be much easier to plan the steps. For more help check out the book by Mager[1].

•*Be specific with the words you use.*
If you look at the "vague" and the "specific" objectives of the example I just gave, you may notice a difference in the verbs used to describe the learner's behavior when performing the result. The latter are **action verbs**; one can actually observe someone doing whatever was set out for them to learn. Rather than appreciating, understanding, having an overview, being exposed to....we use words like compare, list, describe, operate, draw, mix.

•*Communicate your objectives to others.*
Objectives are useful for your work in planning and presenting the course. By sharing them with your learners, you can achieve additional benefits:
   (a) having access to the course objectives, potential learners can make more informed course selection;
   (b) once enrolled, they know what to expect and what is expected of them;
   (c) clearly defined and agreed-upon objectives can become the basis for learning contracts. Students may be given the opportunity to choose certain objectives that suit their needs;
   (d) objectives form the basis for evaluation of student performance, especially in courses where a formal grade must be given at the end;
   (e) outsiders can assess the course more readily by looking over the list of objectives. The final grade becomes less abstract when seen in the context of a list of objectives.

•*Divide objectives according to types of learning.*
Malcolm Knowles[2] provides us with a useful classification of types of objectives, depending on what we are aiming for. The chart on page 9 shows them, with suggested strategies for teaching/learning.

Here is a list of words that can act as triggers to write objectives that describe learner behavior:

Action Verbs:

Creative behavior: ask, change, design, generalize, paraphrase, rewrite, regroup.
Language behavior: abbreviate, edit, spell, pronounce, state, translate.
Artistic behavior: paint, build, carve, draw, illustrate, trace, construct.
Social behavior: discuss, invite, join, contribute, greet, volunteer.
Mathematical behavior: add, calculate, divide, prove, measure, verify, number.
Discriminative behavior: evaluate, infer, compare, decide, analyze, match, order, distinguish, describe.

From a list by C.K. Klaus, in Gronlund, N.E. **Stating Behavioral Objectives for Classroom Instruction.** New York: MacMillan. 1970. pp 53-56.

Step #5 Select Teaching/Learning Strategies...

Teaching someone to swim *by* the lecture method will yield little real learning. A combination of demonstrations, brief lectures, and plenty of practice would be more suitable for this type of learning goal. Yet how many times do instructors lecture for hours on a subject that requires activity, practice, discussion, exploration, questioning, or some other strategy? Certain strategies are more suitable for certain learning objectives. Again, check the chart on page 92.

Step #6 What Resources...

Going through the steps so far may already have brought to mind films, materials, handouts, outside speakers, tools or some other resources that you know of, or hope to be able to locate. Make a list and think ahead. Some films may need to be ordered from out of town, speakers to be contacted to see if they are available (and indeed suitable), supplies to be ordered (and funded), etc.

Step #7 How Will You Know That Learning Is Taking Place?

You and your learners must assess your progress towards the final product. Often a well-written objective provides clues and a basis for evaluation. For example: "The learner will be able to *weigh* and *measure* the ingredients for baking a Sacher Torte, using the *standard devices* and *following the instructions* in the recipe." The *italicized* parts of that statement suggest ways to test through practical written or oral procedures.

Step #8 Make A Tentative Schedule

This step comes in two parts. First, you could sketch out the way you might use the time allotted for the course. Most schools or training programs prescribe the schedule: six hours, five one-hour sessions, 12 three-hour evenings, etc. How do you distribute the learning activities leading to the objectives over the time available? (Allowing space for introductory/warm-up session, evaluation and testing). Second, you could make a more detailed outline for each session. Use the planning form on page 102 to guide you but don't let it limit your creativity.

Step #9 Do It...

There is a certain element of sink-or-swim to this step. While careful planning does not guarantee you stay above water all the time, it certainly gives you the confidence to come up for air at frequent intervals, see where you are going, enjoy the sights a bit, and feel good (if exhausted) when you reach solid ground again at the end.

Step #10 Evaluate. . .

Later in the **KIT** you will find a number of evaluation tools you can use. Ensure they are in your plan! This can be the most important (and exciting) part of the entire process; you can obtain information that either supports what you have been doing or offers opportunity for change and further development. If you haven't done so already, look at Reg Herman's article in the *Resources Section (Creative Decision-Making)*. He makes a case in favour of evaluation at the start, at the end. . .and, in between. The information gathered through evaluation will most likely lead you back to any of the 10 steps just described.

[1]*Malcolm Knowles,* **Self-Directed Learning**. *New York: Association Press. 1975.*

[2]*Robert Mager.* **Preparing Instructional Objectives.** *Palo Alto: Fearon Publ. 1962.*

For other helpful approaches to systematic course planning, see:
Jeorld Kemp. **Instructional Design. A Plan for Unit and Course Development.** *Belmont, CA: Fearon. 1977.*
L.N. Davis & E. McCallon, **Planning, Conducting, Evaluating Workshops.** *Learning Concepts, 1974.*

PLAN-A-LESSON

Course:

Objective(s):

page ___ of ___

Time	What the instructor will do:	What the learners will do:	Teaching aids:
To find out what learners already know:			
To find out what learners have learned:			

The following are basic skills that can be used in any situation where it is important that two or more people understand each other. Adult education events clearly fall into this category! Of the four skills, the first two are best used to help **understand the other person,** while the other two skills allow **others to understand us** better[1].

Skill #1: PARAPHRASING

This can be used to make sure you understand the ideas, information and comments of others. To "paraphrase" means to state the other's idea in your own words, or give an example that shows what you think a person is talking about. A good paraphrase is usually more specific than the original statement was.

Example statement and response:

Diane: "I don't think this course is for me."

Paraphrase A: "You want to change it for another one?"

This is too general and does not reflect what has been said. If Diane agrees with your response and leaves the class you will not know why she felt the course was not for her. You will have an illusion of understanding.

Diane might answer: "No, that's not it. I really want something more practical, not as much theory."

Paraphrase B: "You think it's not for you because it's listed as an advanced course in the calendar?"

This is more specific. This paraphrase leads to a clarification of the way Diane is using the words "Not for me."

Paraphrasing may seem like a bit of extra work and may be awkward for you at first. Why not just get the other person to clarify by asking: "What do you mean?" or by saying, "I don't understand"? Because when you paraphrase, you show what your present level of understanding is and thus enable her to respond to, and clarify, a specific misunderstanding you have revealed.

It sometimes happens that a student comments on or questions something I have said to the class, and I respond quickly with a "Yes, but..." or a "No, you seem to misunderstand me. Let me explain again...." Only after a lengthy explanation (or slightly impatient repetition of my earlier remarks) does the person get a word in edge-wise and say to *me* "You didn't understand my question...!" Therefore, I try to make sure that the remark or comment to which I am responding is really the message the other is sending—*before* I agree or disagree. To paraphrase is one way of testing such understanding.

Skill #2: PERCEPTION CHECKING:

This can be used to make sure you understand the feelings of others. To make a "perception check" means to state what you perceive the other to be feeling. A good perception check conveys the message "I want to understand your feelings—is this [making a statement of his feelings] the way you feel about it?"

Examples:

"Were you disappointed when we didn't follow your suggestion?"

"I get the impression you are annoyed with me, Roger. Are you?"

"You look a bit bewildered. Are you?"

A perception check identifies the other's feelings in some way (disappointed, annoyed, bewildered) and does not express approval or disapproval of the feelings. It merely conveys, "This is how I understand your feelings; am I accurate?"

103

Our inferences about other people's feelings can be, and often are, inaccurate. Thus, if I feel guilty about something I have done, I may perceive others as angry, accusing or disapproving towards me. By remembering to use perception checking I can find out, and I am often surprised at the response.

Skill #3: DESCRIBING BEHAVIOR

This skill is aimed at letting the other person know what behavior you are responding to, by describing it clearly enough that they know what you have observed.

Examples:

"Mark, you seem to take the opposite side of whatever I say today."

NOT, "Mark, you are just trying to show off." [This is not a behavior description but an accusation of unfavourable motives.

"Sue, you have talked more than others on this topic. Several times you have cut others off before they had a chance to speak."

NOT, "Sue, that's rude," which labels and gives no evidence.

NOT, "Sue, you always want to hog the conversation!" which puts her on the spot by implying suspect motives.

"Lois, I don't think John had finished his comment."

NOT, "Lois, you deliberately didn't let John finish." The word "deliberately" implies that Lois knowingly and intentionally cut John off. All one can observe is that she did cut him off.

To develop your skill in describing behavior, you need to sharpen your observation of what actually occurs in the classroom. As you do, you may find that many of your conclusions are based less on observable evidence than on your own feelings of irritation, insecurity, or fear. When I listen to myself making an accusatory statement, I try to listen to the message behind what I am saying; usually there is a feeling that wants expression. If I can let that feeling show, not only do I simplify communication, I also feel much better.

Skill #4: MAKING "I" STATEMENTS (also called BEHAVIOR DESCRIPTION)

This can be useful to help others understand what you are feeling. To make an "I" statement means to make clear what feelings you are experiencing by naming or identifying them. The statement must (a) refer to "I", "me" or "my" and (b) specify some kind of feeling by name or figure of speech.

Because describing feelings ("I" statements) is often confused with expressing feelings, it might help your understanding to give some contrasting examples.

Expression of Feelings	Description of Feelings
"Can't you ever be on time?"	"I've been worried that something happened to you in the traffic."
"Yesterday's session was a flop.'	"I am disappointed about the way I handled yesterday's discussion."
"You are one of my better classes."	"I like working with you. I appreciate that everybody gets a chance to participate."

In addition to expressing feelings through questions, accusations and judgements, we can also show them through non-verbal expressions such as sighing, becoming silent, turning away from the other, keeping the other waiting, etc. Thus, expressions are likely to be misread, since they can come from a number of different feelings and leave the other to guess which is the real message. Describing my feelings (or making "I" statements) should not make someone feel guilty ("Look what you did!") or attempt to coerce them into changing ("So I won't feel bad about your action"). Instead, by reporting what goes on inside me I give you another bit of information that is necessary for you and me to understand each other and develop our relationship.

Based on material by John Wallen

When you ask participants to behave in a certain manner, to operate equipment following certain procedures, or to interact with each other using certain skills, they look to you to set an example. I have caught myself many times sending the confusing message of, "Don't do as I do, do as I say." When learners point out this inconsistency between instructions and behavior, I am reminded of the power of **modeling** as a learning tool.

Modeling can be presented through typed scripts, audio or video recordings, films or by live presentations. The learner's behavior can be changed simply by observing the behavior of others (vicarious learning). The observer need not actually demonstrate the behavior herself. We probably couldn't learn to swim this way but many of our social skills and attitudes were developed by watching "models" (our parents, teachers, friends). The more important the model is perceived to be by the learner, the higher the likelihood that the modeling will have a marked effect.

Typically, teachers are viewed as important by adult learners. We can take advantage of the power of modeling to alter and influence learning. Example: in a class for beginning counselors I first model a certain listening skill and video-record the event. The recording is played back, while I provide cues to focus the trainees' attention on the key elements of the skill. It helps trainees identify the desired behaviors, see how they are used by an experienced counselor, and gives them a mental picture. When they subsequently practice the skill, they can begin by imitating the model. This approach to skills training also gives credibility to the instructor ("Show me if you can do it, before you ask me to make a fool of myself!"). Don't try to be the perfect model, though. Seeing the instructor struggle with a procedure tends to enhance the process, *as long as* you don't take yourself too seriously. Allow yourself to make a mistake—and laugh about it.

Behavior Modeling

Behavior modeling, a part of social-learning theory, can be an effective training tool. Albert Bandura gives several reasons:

Under circumstances in which mistakes are costly or dangerous, skilful performances can be established without needless errors by providing competent models who demonstrate the required activities. Some complex behaviors can be produced solely through the influence of models. If children had no opportunity to hear speech, it would be virtually impossible to teach them the linguistic skills that constitute a language. When desired forms of behavior can be conveyed only by social cues, modeling is an indispensable aspect of learning. Even in instances where it is possible to establish new response patterns through other means, the process of acquisition can be considerably shortened by providing appropriate models.

Bandura, A. **Psychological Modeling.** *New York: Lieber-Atherton. 1971.*

Developing a Sequence of Questions
A 'naturalistic' model
David Tickner, Vancouver Vocational Institute

This model is intended for instructors who wish to generate learner discussion on a subject through the intentional use of questions. It structures interpersonal communication in a natural, productive way. It is "natural" because it follows the path the mind takes when it acknowledges and responds to stimuli. It is "productive" because it leads to decision and action.

The model may seem awkward at first, partly because it requires us to be conscious and purposeful about an activity—communication—which we may prefer to do spontaneously. Another reason is that Western social and educational systems have stressed abstract concepts and theory. When learning or working, we are seldom asked to describe something and/or relate it to our previous experience. We are often asked to evaluate something quickly—a poem, a political system, a person's promotional potential, the source of a problem. We have often been encouraged to "jump the gun" in our communications with others by assuming a mutual knowledge of facts, common images or similar experiences. This frequently leads to poor judgements and misunderstandings based on faulty or incomplete information. For example, instructors will make a presentation and ask learners questions such as: "Well, what do you think about that?" or "How do you feel about that?" and then wonder why no one answers, or why answers seem sporadic and unrelated to one another.

The model consists of a sequence of questions (or statements) at four levels. These enable participants to really look at an event or topic, mull it over, decide their responses to it, and consider courses of action in relation to it.

There are four levels of questions:

1. The Objective Level

The **intent** of this level is to describe or 'recreate' in simple terms the events, object, presentation or situation (i.e. the topic) to be subsequently discussed, and to give all learners a quick chance to participate from the beginning of the session.

Method: Do this step quickly using a variety of short, direct questions. Make sure that everyone has an opportunity to contribute. This level could be called 'getting on stage' or 'clearing the decks for action!'

2. Reflective Level

The **intent** of this level is to call forth the listeners' first impressions and reactions.

Method: Take more time here. Allow people to recall and tell their experiences or feelings. Perhaps not everyone will wish to contribute something. Probe and focus—how did the topic help to illuminate some aspect of one's experience? As the discussion leader, give an illustration from your own experience.

3. Interpretive Level

The **intent** of this level is to provide feedback to the instructor on the impact of the presentation or 'topic' and to examine how the learners perceived its meaning.

Method: Move from a simple recollection of the topic to its impact upon the learners. Focus upon the responses (positive or negative) of the listeners and examine what occasioned these responses.

4. Decisional Level

The **intent** of this level is to enable both the learners and the instructor to go away from the session with fresh insights and resolves as to the future applications of their insights.

Method: This level is done quite quickly, in the nature of a conclusion and a pulling together of the insights of the discussion. It should follow quite naturally from the interpretive level.

The following descriptions and examples form a very basic overview of how the model can be used.

When **preparing** for a session, the instructor may develop several objective-level questions which can be used to stimulate discussion and participation. For example, an instructor might develop 20 objective-level questions and perhaps only two decisional-level ones.

The instructor may also want to describe this 'naturalistic' approach to learners before beginning, in order that the learners anticipate the sequence of questions, and not simply assume that the instructor is beginning the 'traditional' or 'usual' style of discussion.

In a **group discussion**, learners' comments often move back and forth across these levels. Individuals may never move beyond the level of contributing objective information; others may be more concerned with describing their feelings and experiences.

However, the model is most effective when
i) the instructor **begins** the process by encouraging *all* learners to participate by responding to (at the very least) a series of objective-level questions on the subject at hand, and
ii) the instructor **concludes** the session by asking decisional-level questions indirectly or directly to some or all learners. In this way a climate is established in which all learners are invited to participate in the session from the beginning, and where the session ends with some form of closure through which the learners are enabled to see that their participation and learning has been significant and worthwhile.

LEVEL	DESCRIPTION	SAMPLE QUESTIONS
Objective (Facts)	To create a shared picture of the "piece of reality" which is the subject of the discussion To focus attention on what is there To collect data	What examples of 'body language' did you observe? What items caught your attention? What occured in this interview? Who was involved?
Reflective (Associations)	To relate data to individuals' pattern of experience To become aware of related and unrelated information To elicit individuals' reactions to the data	What did this situation remind you of? What were the keywords for you? Was this a helpful exercise for you? Why?
Interpretive (Value)	To consider the meaning of the subject and the individuals' reaction. To build a consensus on the significance of the subject To bring to awareness the impact and/or usefulness of the subject	What *for you* were the most important points clarified? Can you give suggestions for doing this differently? What worked for you? How? Why? Give examples If you had to summarize your learning today and explain it to someone else, what would you say?
Decisional (Action	To accept the challenges which the situation presents To decide what change is necessary To designate specific actions	What do you need to do next to apply what you have learned? What do *we* need to do next? What obstacles can you foresee (in making the change)? How will you know that you have been successful (making the change)?

"Nothing beats a salutation that grabs the audience by the throat, mentions the name or otherwise accurately describes the object of the communication. Napoleon, addressing his massed troops, knew the way: 'Soldiers!'"

William Safire, **What's the Good Word?** New York Times Books. 1982, p. 48.

Much important data that we receive from or give to others consists of feedback related to behavior. Such feedback provides learning opportunities if we use others' reactions to interpret our own behavior.

Such feedback can help you to become more aware of **what** *you do*, **how** you do it and how it all affects your learners. You'll receive ample information based on which you can choose to modify and change your behavior. Your participants in turn can take advantage of the same benefits if given appropriate feedback by you and their peers. Feedback can thus become one of the most meaningful (if often unintended) learning experiences.

Here is a brief outline of things you can do to check and develop your use of feedback as a giver, receiver and model.

Refer to what a person does, rather than what you think he is. Example: "You were very quiet tonight, Linda." NOT: "You are not interested in our discussion, are you?"

Refer to what you see and hear, rather than why thought it happened. Example: "You suddenly went quiet when we talked about life planning." NOT: You are probably afraid to think ten years ahead."

Describe the behavior you are responding to in terms of "more or less" rather than "either/or." Example: Describe someone's participation or performance on a continuum of high to low, rather than "good" to "bad."

Feedback is most useful if given as soon as possible after the observation or reaction. This way the other person can relate it to the facts and emotions of the situation and make better use of the feedback.

Give feedback with the intention of sharing your ideas and information rather than giving advice.

Give just enough information for the other to digest. If you overload the other person with information it reduces the possibility that she may use it effectively. Giving her more than she can use probably satisfies some need of your own rather than helping the other person to learn.

Decide on the value the feedback has for the receiver, not the amount of "release" it will give you. To be classed as "helpful feedback" the information should be something offered, not forced upon the other person.

Feedback does not have to be given verbally. It can be communicated through gestures, eye contact, body stance, and distance between people. However, it is most effective if it comes with an awareness of the above points.

Forms of Interpersonal Feedback[1]

Objective-Descriptive

Describing as clearly as possible the behavior you have seen the other utilize. This does not tell the other the effect of the behavior on you.

> Example: "You have come late to every class we have had so far."

Assumed or Guessed Impact

Revealing your impression of the impact the other's behavior had on a third person. This information may or may not be useful to the recipient.

> Example: "Most people did not understand the point you were trying to make."

Second Party Report of Impact

This is second hand information: feedback pertains to a person's impact on others but it comes from someone not directly involved.

> Example: "Two people came to me after the seminar and told me how well you handled the group discussion."

Direct Descriptive Impact

Probably the most useful kind of feedback: you first describe the other's behavior and then explain your reaction to it.

> Example: "When you took over the discussion I felt relieved."

Direct Evaluation

Labeling the effect of the other's behavior.

> Example: "I feel you like to be in charge of groups."

If this is all the information you receive, it may not be of much help to you. But it can be the starting point in a discussion of *why* the other is perceiving you in this way.

Direct Expressive

This feedback 'sums up' the whole person, yet it is probably triggered by specific behaviors only.

> Example: "You're really a terrific instructor."

The other may be impressed by your smart handling of the flipchart, be flirting with you, or expressing some dissatisfaction with his or her own performance as an instructor. Only an exchange of further information will make this kind of feedback useful to both of you.

Non-Verbal

This data is conveyed by means other than words: the other may nod, smile, close her eyes, doodle, look out the window, frown, tap his pen, yawn. It may be difficult to continue a presentation when most of your listeners are looking out the window. You either plow on because it's only a firetruck getting ready to spray the burning classroom trailer, or you stop and check what's so much more compelling than you. It all depends on your sensitivity and the availability of data in addition to these non-verbal cues.

Performance Reactions

Non-verbal cues are sent not only in form of body language but may also show in the performance of your learners following instruction. The manner in which groups approach your case study assignment may reveal information about the content of the case, the style in which it is written, the way in which you gave the instructions, or the experiences students had with previous case discussions. Again, cues are only hints and require clarification before they can be used more fully.

---

[1]*This is a brief adaptation from an extensive article on the functions and impacts of interpersonal data-sharing by William G. Dyer.* **Training and Development Journal.** *June 1981. 102-109.*

These "leads" are adapted from counseling techniques and are given here in alphabetical order. With some practice you can apply them in a variety of situations.

Recommended To
- assist students in expressing themselves during interviews, in group discussions and during one-to-one encounters
- help you respond with more confidence when presented with students' personal issues.

Acceptance is a non-directive lead through which you show that you are interested in the other and that you understand and accept what she is saying. Don't let your speaking interrupt her momentum and continuity of thought, however. This technique usually involves a simple "yes" or "un-huh," or merely a nod.
Statement: ". . . and I thought that my supervisor would be impressed if I enrolled in this workshop."
Response: "Uh-huh."

Advising is a directive technique in which you tell the other what to do, drawing upon your knowledge and experience to help solve the problem. Advising is similar to urging, but is a milder lead. It may be compared to *Suggestion*, which is a less authoritative way of presenting ideas for the client to consider. A major danger of advising is that it makes it difficult for the other to reject an idea without implying rejection of you, too.
S: "What should I do about getting back into my discussion group?"
R: "I think you should go right up to Miss Jones and apologize."

Approval is a technique through which one person expresses her approval of some particular thing the other has said or done. This technique is used with the hope that the one's approval will influence the behavior of the other. It is used best when the first is an authority on the topic at hand, but it may be dangerous if used indiscreetly or too often.
S: "I think I'll drop out of one of my courses and concentrate on this one alone."
R: "Good! That seems to be a wise decision for you."

Assurance is a lead designed to make the other feel better and to reduce worry about a particular point. It tends to reduce discussion on the point and may be used to help terminate a particular discussion. It may be dangerous, however, in that it tends to transfer responsibility from the other person to you, thereby restricting self-insight. It should be used only when you have a specific purpose in mind and have considered the possible negative results. Continued or repeat use of this technique tends to reduce tension or concern and might be labeled "reassurance."
S: "I guess I worry too much about passing my level III exam."
R: "Yes, you are probably doing better than you think."

Clarification is used to help clear up your own thinking as to what the other means. It also gives him a chance to see how well someone else understands him, and provides an opportunity for him to correct any misunderstanding. In this technique, you verbalize what you think the other is trying to say. Avoid intellectualizing or changing the content of his expressions. He can see his own statements in a less personal light.

S: "My wife shouldn't have to work so hard. My training isn't that important."

R: "You mean your wife is sacrificing her needs to yours?"

Clarification-semantic has the same general purpose as the clarification technique above and is designed to deal especially with obvious semantic problems such as extensive use of slang or with bilingual conflicts. It is useful in helping you to understand terminology which may be quite familiar to the other but foreign to your vocabulary.

S: "Yeah, she think's she's pretty cool!"

R: "You mean she thinks she knows more about this than you do?"

Deliberate misinterpretation is a lead technique designed to force the other to talk about her problems. It may be dangerous unless rapport has been fairly well established. Using this technique you deliberately mistake what the other has said or implied, in order to make her realize that she is not expressing herself clearly. This usually has the result of forcing the other to go into more detail in an attempt to be understood.

S: "I can't seem to get excited about Mr. Smith's course—he just leaves me cold."

R: "You mean you don't think he knows what he's talking about?"

Evaluation is a technique designed to help the client see the relative values of certain alternatives. It is used to encourage self-insight and self-planning and is most effective when dealing with problems of decisions about courses of action. Evaluation usually involves a series of leads designed to draw out both sides of a question and to balance these arguments against each other. Evaluation leads are frequently used near the end of a 'conference' to stimulate further contemplation of a problem afterwards.

S: "I don't know whether I really should go for the diploma!"

R: "What might be some of the advantages if you did? [or disadvantages?]"

General Leads usually take the form of questions or statements intended to get the other to shift his thinking to a different aspect of his problem. At the beginning of a conversation they may serve to suggest a topic for discussion or, at the close, they may call attention to a related aspect of the problem. They frequently follow a *Summary Clarification* or they may be used to break a long silence. The actual lead itself may take the form of "probing," "suggestion," or some other lead designed to stimulate consideration of a new aspect of the situation.

S: "Well, I guess that's a pretty good picture of my situation."

R: "Let's see, you also mentioned some problems with the essay, didn't you."

Illustration-personal is a technique in which you use an example involving your own experience to illustrate a particular point and to convince the other that you are sympathetic and understanding. This technique does not promote a better understanding of another and his problem since he or she is likely to feel obligated to some extent to accept the point you are trying to make. It does not give the other the necessary freedom of choice without risking a personal offense to you.

S: "I wish I knew how to tell this to my other instructor."

R: "I often find it difficult to discuss such things with my boss. The last time I just went in, told him how difficult it was for me to discuss this with him, and then . . . ."

A second **Illustration-personal** is a technique in which you can set up an example involving a third person. Like the preceding technique involving illustration, this is meant to suggest ideas and courses of action appropriate to the other's problems. However, this technique is less dangerous to use, since the other is free to accept or reject the ideas without fear of hurting anyone's feelings. Even though you are relating a personal experience, the use of the third person avoids personal implications.

> **S:** "I wish I knew how to tell this to my other instructor."
> **R:** "During the last course a student had a similar situation and he . . ."

Incomplete thought is a technique in which you deliberately pause in the middle of a sentence to see if the other will complete it. This technique is used to draw out the other's thinking about a particular point which seems important to you.

> **S:** "He and I just don't get along, so what's the point?"
> **R:** "Because things didn't go well in the past, you feel . . . ."

Informing is used as a lead in order to convey information with which the other may be unfamiliar and may have a bearing on his problem. This technique is used most frequently when providing education or occupational information.

> **S:** "Where could I find out about professional training?"
> **R:** "You could call the Association and ask them to send you the calendar."

Interpretation is a lead technique in which you state something which can be inferred from what the other has just said *and* from your knowledge of (or personal information related to) the problem. Interpretation accelerates the development of insight and causes little difficulty if rapport is well established and the other person is sincere. Interpretation can cause resistance, however, if your remark is too far ahead of the other's own thinking or if it threatens his concept of self and security.

> **S:** "If I could only get some experience in this field, my chances for employment after this course would be much better."
> **R:** [Knowing that the student has not been able to keep two previous jobs in this field] "But you're not sure if this course really *will* make a difference, or if you'll just end up where you started from?"

Moralizing is a technique in which you try, directly or indirectly, to help the other relate moral or ethical values to her plan of action. If rapport is well established, this may be effective in developing better concepts of self-in-society, but if handled poorly, may meet with considerable resistance and break down rapport. Be very careful in using this technique and consider the outcomes carefully before attempting it.

> **S:** "With this self-evaluation someone could just give himself top marks."
> **R:** [Directive] "But that wouldn't be in the spirit of an honest evaluation."
> *or*
> [Non-directive] "But who'd be cheating whom?"

Probing is one of *the* most directive techniques and involves asking a series of direct questions for the purpose of getting information about the other or his problem. Excessive use of probing may cause resistance and destroy rapport. Be particularly cautious about using it too much early in a relationship.

> **S:** "I am not sure why I am taking this workshop."
> **R:** "What do you mean, you're not sure?"
> **S:** "I have been a supervisor for three years, so why do I have to take "supervisory skills"?"

117

R: "Why *are* you here?"
S: "I was told to be here, Monday morning 9 a.m."
R: "Who told you?"
S: "Hagen in Personnel."
R: "What else were you told by Mr. Hagen?"
S: "He talked about my performance review last month."
R: "How did that work out. . .?"

Projection-interpersonal is a technique in which you try to get the other to see his problem situation from someone else's viewpoint. You might ask him to play a particular role, not as himself, but as he thinks it would be played by a particular individual. Insight through projection is seldom accomplished by the use of a single lead. You must hold the other in the projected position for several leads in order to clarify his perspective and develop insight.

S: "I just can't see why Bert's group can't be a bit more flexible."
R: "If you were to put yourself in Bert's position, how would *you* feel about these changes?"

Projection-time is a technique in which the instructor tries to get the individual to project himself into the future or review the past to get a different perspective on the problem. This technique serves to give both parties better insight into possible causes or effects of the issues under discussion. Projection into the future is appropriate when some clarification of future goals is essential as a basis for current motivations. It may be tricky when used to review the past, as it may uncover aspects of the other's problem which you are incapable of handling. Therefore, it should be used cautiously by the inexperienced. As with the technique above, you must structure a series of leads designed to hold the other at the projected period for sufficient time to develop understanding. Projections slip back into the present very easily if the initiator does not maintain a careful control of the structure during the use of this lead technique.

S: [After a successful presentation during an instructional skills workshop]
"I wish I could do this as well when I am with my real trainees."
R: "Why don't you take a moment, Terry—look back to the last time things didn't go well. Could you tell us what happened?"
or
"Try this. Imagine yourself in your next training session. How would you set things up with *your* students to ensure success?"

Reflection of feeling is a non-directive technique in which you try to describe the attitude of the other. This technique is used in order to bring feelings to the surface and to get more verbalization by the other. Thus it serves to bring issues into focus without the other feeling that he is being probed or pushed by the listener.

S: "I wish I could talk to fellow-workers like this, but it never seems to come out the right way."
R: "You are a bit frustrated with your way of communicating with the people in your department?"

Selective reflection is a valuable technique for keeping a discussion going. From a group of thoughts or attitudes expressed by the other, you select one and verbalize it with the hope of stimulating further exploration of the problem. You draw on your knowledge of previous encounters with this person in selecting ideas which seem to need clarification. In this way, you can direct the discussion without the other being aware of it. When handled skilfully, the technique makes the other feel that he initiated all of the points discussed.

S: "...of course, I have been very busy during the last few weeks and I have spent quite a bit of time on my project, but I just don't seem to get the hang of it."

R: [Being aware that the other has had to work on a special sales promotion at work] "You've been very busy?"

Simple restatement is the technique of acting as a mirror for verbal expression. In this technique you merely restate exactly the other's last words in an attempt to help her realize how she sounds. This often encourages her to expand and to clarify her remarks.

S: "...but I am not sure just what is expected of me."

R: "You are not sure what is expected of you...."

Silence is the technique by which you can encourage others to comment further by remaining completely silent and waiting for them to go on.

S: "One thing I got from this course was a new view of myself as a participant in meetings."

R: _____

Suggestion is a less directive way of supplying ideas to the other than is advising. Try to inject some possible courses of action into the other's thinking without telling him what to do. Although a difficult technique to master. it has very positive value in encouraging self-direction and self-discipline. It supplies ideas in such a way that the other feels free to explore them and to accept or reject them without offending the sender.

S: "I am stuck. I just can't come up with a thesis topic. There are so many possibilities!"

R: "Have you thought of writing all the topics that interest you on little cards, and then... "[explains a decision-making technique]

Summary clarification is used at the end of a series of remarks on some topic in order to organize and summarize for the other what has been said. This technique should be used after you feel that his particular aspect of the problem has been discussed adequately. It may close the discussion of the problem at hand, or the client may take up additional points which he thinks are important.

S: "I can't think of any more."

R: "Let's see if we have the whole picture then. We talked about...and you feel that.... Is that about the way you see it?"

Urging is a directive technique similar to and often following _Advising_. Here you try to get the other to follow a particular course of action. It often includes your personal solutions to problems and reflects your values. Phrases like "why don't you" and "you should" often occur. Urging can be used effectively when the respondent is an authority in a particular field, but it can lead to much resistance or to passive acceptance without any will to attempt a solution. Consider carefully the possible reactions of the other before undertaking this lead.

S: "I suppose I ought to just go back and level with the others."

R: "Yes, you should. Why don't you go back, ask for a moment of your group's time and tell them how you feel. They'll be able to understand your action better—and you'll probably feel relieved."

Do you want to know what participants think of your efforts? Do you want them to share their suggestions for improvements? On the following pages are a number of instruments which you can use as they are, or change to suit your needs. Just be gentle on yourself—balance your questions so that you may receive positive *and* negative comments. Receiving more of one or the other gives you a false picture and may also affect your self-image.

•Allow time for the completion of your evaluation in class. I have not been successful with evaluations which participants take home or have sent to them after their workshop. The return rate is zilch unless, perhaps, you offer free trips to Reno.

•Share the collected information with the group and process it. A summary of comments on a piece of newsprint shows that you care about what's been written and aren't afraid to deal with issues. Participants also get a feel for others' opinions and can see their own in context.

•Do evaluations at more than one point in a course. Even comments received halfway through a one-day seminar can often be considered during the rest of the day's proceedings. The problem with end-of-course evaluations is that you have no way of sharing the information, no way of implementing suggestions, no way of getting additional information on incomplete statements.

•Keep your evaluations. Look at them when you plan a repeat performance and include whichever suggestions you feel comfortable with. Also, use past evaluations to measure your own development. You *are* getting better!

•If you need information on the evaluation of "content," as in tests, quizzes and examinations, see:

Gronlund, N. **Constructing Achievement Tests**. *Englewood Cliffs, NJ: Prentice Hall.*

Green, J.A. **Teacher-made Tests**. *New York: Harper & Row, 1963.*

Priestley, M. **Performance Assessment in Education & Training**. *Englewood Cliffs, NJ: Educational Technology Publ. 1982.*

This questionnaire was developed for a group leadership course where the emphasis was on leadership and participation skills. Respondents are asked to rate themselves on the nature of their interaction with others. The information gathered can be used for a class discussion on common difficulties as well as to provide cues for instructor input of theory. A "symbol" is used here instead of student's name; sometimes anonymous responses are given more freely. People can always "own" their comments during the discussion period.

LEARNING SELF—EVALUATION CHECKLIST

Symbol_____

	very little	some-what	occas-ionally	quite a lot
Were you interested in this unit?	_____	_____	_____	_____
Did you learn "content"?	_____	_____	_____	_____
Did you learn "process"?	_____	_____	_____	_____
Did you learn about your own behavior?	_____	_____	_____	_____
Did you participate?	_____	_____	_____	_____
Did you assume "maintenance" roles?	_____	_____	_____	_____
Did you assume "task" roles?	_____	_____	_____	_____

List below three personal learning goals which you have after today's session:
　　　　"I want to . . . ."

1.

2.

3.

VARIATION

To obtain more specific information, ask participants to give one example for each of the categories above. Rather than just checking off an item, they now have to support their choice of rating. This specifying can also be done in small-group discussions after each has completed the checklist.

This questionnaire was designed for a specific part of a "group dynamics" course. Participants are asked to comment on their performance in the group, assess it in the context of the group's overall task, and give the instructor suggestions for change. This form reflects the mutual respect between learners and the instructor.

AFTER THE DISCUSSION

We have talked about **roles** people assume during discussion sessions and how some of these are helpful to the process, while others are hindering.

What role(s) did you assume most of the time today?

Comment on the helpfulness of your contributions.

What is your personal reaction to today's sessions?

What problems do you see in the group?

How can the instructor help?

What could you do to help the group?

_____
Signed

This is the most versatile of all. It can be filled out at various stages of the course. It concentrates on high and low points and asks the respondent to give reasons for each rating.

DAILY QUESTIONNAIRE

1. What do you consider to have been today's most valuable experience?

   Why?

2. What aspect of today's program could have been strengthened?

   How?

3. Any additional comments?

                              Your name _____

                                        optional

Another variation using the unfinished sentence technique to obtain quite personal information about the course the its direction.

HALF WAY THROUGH...

Our course is half finished and this is a good point to stop and see how we are doing. I am particularly interested in your views on the way each week's session is structured, my own performance, and your feeling about the usefulness of it all.

Please complete the sentences below.

1. The structure of our sessions is...

    I wish...

2. I like least about your performance...

    and wish you...

3. I wish we did more...

4. I wish we did less...

5. With only five sessions remaining we should...

6. If I had to sum up my feelings about the way this course is going, I would say...

_____
Signed

The first session together in a new group can be overwhelming for many participants. This form asks them to look back over the event, report their feelings and impressions at various stages, and summarize the highlights. The instructor can use the same form. An open discussion arising from this questionnaire can air information which would otherwise be missed.

OUR FIRST SESSION TOGETHER

Please finish the sentences below so that I can get a feel for what this evening was like for you.

When I first walked into the room . . .

Now that the session is over I wish . . .

My first impression of the instructor was . . .

The get-acquainted activity was . . .

The way we were asked to write down our learning needs . . .

The small group activities were . . .

My overall feeling towards this group is . . .

_____

Signed

Thank You and Good Night

On this form participants are asked to rate a series of statements and briefly explain their choice of response [Customer Relations Course].

EVALUATING TODAY'S LEARNING

Name: _____

Please take a few minutes at the end of this session to reflect on what has just happened in this room. By responding honestly to the questions below, you can give me valuable information which I can use to plan future sessions. You'll also help me grow as an instructor.

		Not at all	Some-what	Very much
1.	I found the session enjoyable.	_____	_____	_____
2.	The structure of the session was right.	_____	_____	_____
3.	The pace suited me.	_____	_____	_____
4.	Everyone had a chance to participate.	_____	_____	_____
5.	I felt respected.	_____	_____	_____
6.	The examples given were good.	_____	_____	_____
7.	The role play was a good way to learn about assertiveness.	_____	_____	_____
8.	The film helped me understand the idea of "personal space."	_____	_____	_____
9.	Because of the session I am going to experiment with my own assertive behavior.	_____	_____	_____
10.	I am looking forward to next week's session.	_____	_____	_____

Please use this space to give additional comments to make the next session effective and enjoyable.

A Quiz:

How do you think a large sample of North Americans rated the following answers to the question: "Why do adults choose to learn on their own instead of taking a course?" There are 10 questions, rank each by inserting a number between 1 and 10.

- ☐ want to set my own structure on the learning project.
- ☐ don't like formal classroom situation with a teacher.
- ☐ want to use my own style of learning.
- ☐ don't know of any class that offers what I want to learn.
- ☐ don't have enough money to attend a course.
- ☐ transportation to class is a problem.
- ☐ want to set my own pace.
- ☐ want to keep the learning strategy flexible and easy to change.
- ☐ haven't got the time to engage in group learning.
- ☐ want to learn this right away and can't wait until a course might start.

(Answers: 2, 8, 3, 6, 9, 10, 1, 4, 7, 5)

Source:
Penland, P. **"Individual Self-planned Learning in America."** U.S. Office of Education, Office of Libraries and Learning. 1977. p. 32.

The Experiential Learning Cycle

David Kolb, a developmental psychologist, has developed a way of looking at adult learning as an "experiential process"[1]. Learning for him is a four-stage cycle: concrete experience (CE), reflective observation (RO), abstract conceptualization (AC), and active experimentation (AE).

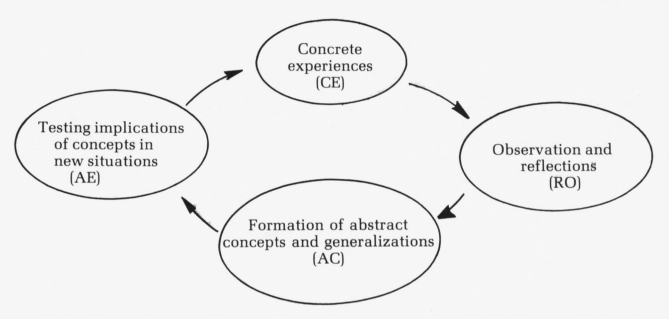

A learner, to be fully effective, needs four different abilities. She must be able to involve herself fully, openly, and without bias in new experiences (CE), she must be able to reflect on and observe these experiences from many perspectives (RO), she must be able to create concepts that integrate her observations into logically sound theories (AC), and she must be able to use these theories to make decisions and solve problems (AE).

To state it another way[2], learning can be seen as a process in which a person experiences something directly, not vicariously, reflects on the experience as something new or as related to other experiences, develops some concept by which to name the experience, and uses the concept in subsequent actions as a guide for behavior. Out of these four steps the person derives a new set of experiences that lead to a repeat of the learning cycle.

---

[1]Kolb has developed a Learning Styles Inventory (see next page) and written extensively on the use of learning styles information in problem-solving, career planning, and course development. A good place to start reading is: Kolb, D. & Fry, R. "Toward an Applied Theory of Experiential Learning," in G. Cooper [ed.] **Theories of Group Process.** London: Wiley. 1975.

[2]How might you apply the experiential learning model in field projects, practica and internships? For suggestions see: Glen L. Gish. "The Learning Cycle." **Synergist.** Spring 1979. pp 2-6.

Self-Reports of Training Outcome

A technique commonly used to measure trainees' progress in a course is to have them complete pre-post evaluation forms. Individuals thus evaluate their skills, knowledge and attitudes with respect to the course content both at the outset and at the conclusion of a training event. A typical question on a self-report might be:

My ability to manage my time at work

1   2   3   4   5   6   7

ineffective   very effective

The trainee is instructed to place an X at the point on the scale which best describes her level of functioning prior to training and after the training to place an O at the level then. To analyse the results, the instructor (and trainee) compare the pre- and post-test results to see where significant changes occurred.

Recently, this traditional self-reporting method has been criticized as being inaccurate for two reasons: 1) Participants have difficulty assessing what they have learned and therefore underestimate training benefits; 2) Participants may think that they learned more than they actually did and therefore overestimate training benefits. Researchers[1] refer to "Response-Shift Bias" as the reason: the tendency for a trainee to revise his/her internal standard for judging him/herself as a result of exposure to training.

To overcome this bias, Pre-Then-Post testing is recommended and has resulted in improved assessment results in several studies[2]. The quickest way to explain this is to show how instructions to the trainee might look on a post-test questionnaire:

INSTRUCTIONS FOR ADMINISTRATION OF THE THEN INSTRUMENT

This questionnaire gives you the chance to re-evaluate your skill level before the training began. Think back to the beginning of this program. Now that the training is over, how would you rate yourself as having been before?

You may remember how you rated yourself on these skills when you took the pretest at the beginning. *Do not* simply tell us (from memory) how you *used* to see yourself. Rather, we want these ratings to be your current opinion of how you *should* have rated yourself (in light of your new understanding or awareness of yourself). There *may or may not* be any difference between your old pretest rating and this re-evaluated one. Don't worry about whether your re-evaluated ratings agree or disagree with your earlier ones.

Your results will not be seen by the ABC Corporation and your answers will be kept strictly confidential. So please answer as honestly as possible.

---

[1]B. Mezoff. *"How to get Accurate Self-Reports of Training Outcomes."* **Training & Development Journal.** *September 1981, pp 56-61.*

[2]*Bob Mezoff's article cites studies that demonstrate the effectiveness of Pre-Then-Post testing in several training settings: interviewing skills training, basic helping skills, assertiveness training and improvement in teaching skills.*

Consider Learning Styles When Planning Programs

"Learning style" is the unique way each individual gathers and processes information. By understanding these differences and taking them into consideration when designing any type of educational program, you can have more effective learning outcomes, more positive learner participation, and even reduce training time[1]. Kolb's Learning Styles Inventory[2] has been developed to measure a person's learning style. This is a self-rating assessment of the learner's perceived preference for concrete versus abstract learning and for active versus reflective learning.

David Kolb and his associates have tested the LSI on a number of different groups, such as managers, college students, medical students, and college faculty. The results helped identify four statistically different types of learning styles, which Kolb has designated as "Converger, Diverger, Assimilator, and Accommodator." Their characteristics are summarized below.

CONVERGER

The Converger's learning style emphasizes abilities in Abstract Conceptualization (AC) and Active Experimentation (AE). An individual with this learning style seems to do best in activities requiring the practical application of ideas. His knowledge seems to be organized so that through hypothetical deductive reasoning he may focus it on specific problems. Research has shown Convergers to be relatively unemotional, having a preference for working with "things" rather than people, and having narrow technical interests, generally choosing to specialize in engineering and physical sciences.

DIVERGER

The Diverger has a learning style opposite to that of the Converger, with strength in imaginative ability and being able to view complex situations from many perspectives. He performs well in "brainstorming" sessions. Research has shown Divergers to be interested in people, having broad cultural interests often specializing in the arts. This style of learning is characteristic of humanities and liberal arts programs. Counselors, personnel managers, and sociologists tend toward this style.

ASSIMILATOR

The Assimilator's dominant learning abilities are Abstract Conceptualization (AC) and Reflective Observation (RO). Persons with this learning style excel in the creation of theoretical models and inductive reasoning. Although he is concerned with the practical use of theories, it is more important to the Assimilator that the theory be logically sound; and if the theory does not fit the "facts," he is likely to re-examine those facts. This learning style is more characteristic of persons in the basic sciences and mathematics than the applied sciences.

ACCOMMODATOR

The Accommodator's learning strengths lie in doing things and involving oneself in new experiences. Quite the opposite of the Assimilator, this person excels in situations where he must adapt to specific immediate circumstances, and if his plan or theoretical explanation does not fit the situation, he will discard it. He tends to solve problems in an intuitive, trial and error manner, relying on others for information instead of his own analytic ability. The Accommodator is at ease with people and often found in action-oriented jobs in business, marketing or sales.

The most obvious use for the Inventory is for the purpose of pre-course planning. It could be mailed to participants several weeks before the first meeting, returned to the planner, scored and the results used to plan the instructional techniques, learner activities and teaching aids. Scores could be averaged and the event tailored to meet the needs of the majority. Or, the group could be divided according to learning style similarities—or differences.

An alternative use is to correlate it with course evaluations. For example, a person who did not like the use of discussion and small group activities (and had a high score on Abstract Conceptualization), probably did so because he or she prefers theory, symbols and logical thinking over people-oriented activities and discovery-type learning. This combined information makes better use of participants' comments than a mere "0" rating on "How did you like the group projects?"

You could also use the survey's information for deliberately not "matching." The most effective learning may occur when the learner is confronted with new, uncomfortable environments that elicit the application or development of nondominant learning abilities[4].

[1]The Learning Style Inventory (self-scoring booklet, $2.50; technical manual, $10.00) may be ordered from McBer and Company, 136 Newbury Street, Boston, MA. 02116.

[2]Nancy Dixon. "Incorporating Learning Style Into Training Design." **Training & Development Journal.** July 1982. pp 62-64.

[3]Adapted by Pigg, K.E. et al. "Learning Styles in Adult Education: A Study of County Extension Agents." **Adult Education.** 30 (4) 1980, 233-244.

[4]Ronald Fry & David Kolb. "Experiential Learning Theory and Learning Experiences in Liberal Arts Education." **New Directions for Experiential Learning.** San Francisco: Jossey-Bass. 1979. pp 79-91.

Subject Index

ORDER FORM

TRAINING ASSOCIATES LTD.

P.O. Box 58246 Station "L"
Vancouver, B.C. V6P 6E3
Canada
(604) 263-7091

Please send me the following books by Peter Renner:

QTY.	PRODUCT TITLE	UNIT PRICE	TOTAL PRICE
	The Instructor's Survival Kit	US $19.95	
	The (Quick) Instructional Planner	CD $20.95	
	Order amount $		
	Add shipping rate on order amount $		
	AMOUNT OWING $		

SHIPPING RATES per book:

US $		CAN $	
bookrate	airmail	bookrate	airmail
2.50	4.50	1.50	4.25

Bookrate: Takes between 4 and 6 weeks to reach you.
Airmail: Takes between 1 and 2 weeks to reach you.
We ship within 2 working days of receiving your order.

PAYMENT METHOD:

☐ I enclose a check/cheque for $_____
☐ Charge my ☐ VISA ☐ MasterCard

Credit
Card # ☐☐☐☐ ☐☐☐☐ ☐☐☐☐ ☐☐☐☐

Expiration
date ☐☐ / ☐☐   Number above
name on MC ☐☐☐

Signature _____

SHIP TO:

_____
NAME

_____
TITLE

_____
DEPARTMENT

_____
COMPANY

_____
STREET

_____
CITY

_____
STATE/PROVINCE

_____
ZIP/POSTAL CODE

FURTHERMORE:

☐ Please send me details on the Workshop Manuals by Training Associates.

I am interested in:
☐ Basic Training Skills
☐ Basic Communications Skills
☐ Conflict Resolution

☐ I have these comments about The "Kit":

_____
_____
_____
_____
_____
_____
_____

YOU MAY QUOTE ME.   ☐ YES   ☐ NO

GUARANTEE:

You may return any book for a full refund if you find it unsatisfactory!